FINDING *the* BRIGHT SIDE

FINDING *the* BRIGHT SIDE

The Art of Chasing What Matters

SHANNON BREAM

CONVERGENT
New York

Published in the United States by Convergent Books, an imprint of the Crown Publishing Group, a division of Penguin Random House LLC, New York.
convergentbooks.com

CONVERGENT BOOKS is a registered trademark and its C colophon is a trademark of Penguin Random House LLC.

Library of Congress Cataloging-in-Publication data is available upon request.

ISBN 978-1-5247-6347-3
Ebook ISBN 978-1-5247-6349-7

Printed in the United States of America

Jacket design by Jessie Sayward Bright
Jacket photograph: Barry Morgenstein

10 9 8 7 6 5 4 3 2

First Edition

To my momma, for giving me the strongest wings
and my beloved Sheldon, for making me believe I could actually fly

Contents

FINDING *the* BRIGHT SIDE

Introduction

My voice cracked as I looked out into the packed auditorium and tried to gather my thoughts. I was frightened and exhausted, scanning the crowd and hoping to catch a glimpse of support from my mother. "God, please help me," I whispered under my breath. But I couldn't see my mother's face. I couldn't see *any* faces, or the clock at the back of the room that was supposed to help me pace my speech and wrap up on time. It was all a blurry mess.

Weeks earlier I'd finally had the cornea surgery I'd been putting off for years. The procedure was the best bet I had at finding some relief from a long-running case of chronic pain. My vision should've healed, and actually improved from before, within a couple of weeks of the operation. But here I was, long past the time my vision should have returned, and no one could explain why my corneas weren't healing. I couldn't drive and was struggling to make sense of the blurry images on my phone and computer. At work, where I normally roamed the halls asking everyone about their weekends and complimenting their outfits, I now spent most of the day hiding in my office. My world felt like it was closing in on me, and I was losing hope.

It had been a taxing journey just getting to the auditorium. People laughed nervously when I referred to my mother as my "seeing-eye human," but I meant it literally. At the airport on the way here, I couldn't see more than a few feet ahead of me and had to depend on the kindness of strangers to find the right gate. I cried more than once, terrified that I'd spend the rest of my life visually impaired and needy.

Surely the organizer would understand if I canceled, right? I felt miserable, with no idea how I'd deliver what the audience had been promised: an uplifting, inspiring speech on two of the great joys in my life—my faith and my work. Just days ahead of the event, I had dissolved into tears with my husband. "I'm a disaster right now," I sobbed. "How am I supposed to stand up there and offer anything hopeful to all these people?"

All I wanted was permission to bow out from the event. Instead, his answer was simple. "Tell the truth."

I've spent most of my life trying to make sure the outside world saw someone who had it together. Even when it made no sense to pretend, I kept a smile on my face and acted like all was well. Law degree with honors? Check. Perfect husband and marriage? Check. Flourishing career? Check. Deep faith? Check. Instagrammable travels around the world? Double check. Yet all that desperate striving required an enormous expenditure of energy. Now I was onstage with no cover: as exposed and as vulnerable as I had ever been.

I said a prayer, summoned my courage, and told the audience exactly how I felt.

"The truth is, I'm in a really tough place right now," I said. "I had a surgery weeks ago, and my recovery isn't going well. I feel overwhelmed and afraid. There are plenty of things I don't understand, but I do know this: what's happening now will make sense in the future."

I couldn't read anyone's face to see if my honesty was connecting or landing with a thud. This wasn't my usual lighthearted speech, full of self-deprecating humor and punch lines. It was raw and gritty. But I knew I'd done what I was supposed to do.

At the end of the speech, I found my way offstage and reconnected with my mom, relieved that it was over. What happened next was an overwhelming surprise. People lined up down the aisles, waiting to hug me, to pray with me on the spot, and to share their own pain. I lost track of time. There were plenty of tears, yet I was flooded with a wave of encouragement that swallowed all the pain of the last month. I was depressed and hurting, and that stage had been the last place I wanted to be. But what I got in return for taking off my mask was immeasurable—genuine connections with other people who had been down similar paths. Their love and prayers sustained me as my recovery continued.

That night taught me something that's taken decades to really understand. Life is an adventure, and I've loved most of it as much as my beloved Disney World—full of princess fantasies and scary rides. My mom actually visited the Central Florida attraction when she was pregnant with me, a trip she believes sparked my lifelong addiction to the Electric Light Parade and endless rounds of "It's a Small World" (which, to be fair, can send even the most tolerant parent over the edge). I've got pictures of me in mouse ears with my dad as I ran through the entry gates, him in his polyester 1970s pants and me in a sundress without a care in the world.

That's how I generally see life, full of good things around every corner. But like everyone, I've fought past crushing moments of embarrassment. I've rallied after falling down the stairs at a lieutenant governor's Christmas party, or earlier in life, after failing to make the varsity cheerleading squad. (How else would I have gotten that varsity letter for warming the volleyball team's bench?) I've acknowledged questionable on-air wardrobe choices and deleted tweets I'd like to pretend never existed. There have been darker moments, too. Whether it was getting fired from my first news job by a boss who told me, "You're the worst person I've ever seen on TV," or hearing the words, "There's no cure," I've walked through the same deep valleys everyone else has. And yet, I still drive my coworkers crazy with my nonstop singing and my insistence on calling it "Fri-yay!" Because in the end, through all the darkness and light—there is joy.

I don't know if I was born seeing the world that way, or if it's a coping mechanism I learned from the crazy things I've lived through. All I know is this: life is unpredictable and short and funny. It just is. Sometimes all you can do is learn to laugh at yourself and believe other people—whether senators or snarky baristas—can be won over with kindness.

Every day I'm on a mission to make curmudgeons smile, like the terrifying boss I had when I interned on Capitol Hill. On day one, as soon as the congressman left the office, the chief of staff barked at me, "Get General So-and-So on the phone now!" Remember, kids, this was preinternet, and I was pretty sure I couldn't just pull out the white pages and find the direct line to top military brass. As I looked around at my new coworkers, the chief of staff added, "Anyone who helps her is fired!"

By the end of the summer, though, I realized my boss was human. I was pretty sure he wouldn't *actually* murder anyone, and I kept showing up every day—smiling as he yelled in my direction. I think on my final day he might have smiled back, maybe. And I did end up tracking down that general's phone number—even without Google.

Along the way, I've discovered plenty about people, including myself. I've learned what it means to find peace in who you are and the life you actually lead. I couldn't have planned or anticipated the best or worst moments of my life. But I've come to feel grateful for them all, because each one has taught me something I wouldn't have learned any other way.

"Meanest Mom in the World"

Not many eleven-year-olds look forward to spending a sunny Saturday afternoon touring a time-share property with their parents. But I wasn't your normal tween, and I had a very specific reason for accompanying my parents on their path toward fractional real estate ownership: a Sony Walkman.

Weeks earlier, a letter had arrived inviting my parents to a ONCE-IN-A-LIFETIME OPPORTUNITY! In exchange for giving up a few hours on a weekend, they would be granted their choice of several prizes, including that Walkman. It was 1982, and I was convinced I needed one.

I grew up in a very strict household, where secular music was forbidden. If we didn't sing it at church, it was pretty much off-limits in the Norris home. However, after a summer spent hanging out with the cool kids across the street, I'd managed to develop a taste for the forbidden tunes of '80s artists like Lionel Ritchie and Chicago. (You know, real edgy stuff.) As soon as my parents got that letter, I knew the Walkman was my ticket to getting a fix.

That meant I was willing to put up with a lot, including spending the better part of a Saturday with a very determined salesman who regaled my parents with tales of how our ownership week at a modest beachfront property along Florida's southeast coast could be traded for glorious vacations in Hawaii and Europe. Even at that age, the proposition seemed dicey to me. But I digress . . .

With my Walkman finally secured, I would stay up late under the covers on Sunday nights listening to Casey Kasem's Top 40 countdown, safely out of earshot from Mom. I always felt a chill of excitement when Kasem said, "Coming to you from Hollywood!" at the top of each segment. My family lived in Pembroke Pines, just down the street from Hollywood, Florida, and I couldn't believe Mr. Kasem was doing such important work just miles from my home. (Years later, Kasem was one of my judges at the Miss USA Pageant. I resisted the urge to share this middle-school confessional with him.)

The Walkman was just part of the sneaky behavior I employed to live peaceably under the same roof as my mom, a woman who once bought a plaque with the words *Meanest Mom in the World* and proudly hung it in the kitchen. She meant it. In my mother's household, hit shows like the *Love Boat* and *Three's Company* were "not appropriate for nice little girls." So was the prospect of staying up past 8:00 p.m.—and don't even *think* about talking back.

There was no escaping from Mom's rule, especially because she worked as a teacher and always taught at the school I attended. Looking back on the experience, I can see how it kept me out of a lot of trouble (a fact for which I'm now eternally grateful). But at the time it was a soul-crushing arrangement for someone who already had to fight hard to fit in. Grade school is fraught enough with potential humiliation when your mom's not correcting you in front of your classmates, or handing out detentions to your friends like Halloween candy.

In fourth grade, one fateful interaction left me with no choice but to run away from home with my friend Michelle. Mom had been passing through the gymnasium just after my class finished recess. The school's rules required us to wear dresses every day (long pants for the boys), so I don't remember there being much physical exertion on the playground. But on this particular day, my mom spotted my messy hair from across the room and came over to whip it back into shape. I was mortified.

I remember protesting that I would look like a baby if my mom started fixing my ponytail in front of my friends, but she was undeterred. "Stand up straight!" she said, fussing over my unruly tresses while my peers stared and snickered. That was the final straw!

Later that day, as Michelle and I discussed our parents' overbearing behavior, we decided to fight back. We both had bikes, and there was a park not far from our school. We figured we could squirrel away some snacks, write good-bye notes, and disappear to the park for just a single day. Maybe that would scare our parents enough to respect our maturity and ability to make our own decisions.

As we planned our big escape, we felt like secret agents, real adults. And if our mothers hadn't still done our laundry at that point in life, we might've gotten away with it. Though I had carefully counseled Michelle over where she should hide her note until we were ready to drop our bomb, she had done her own thing. One day, when her mother went to restock her sock drawer—we were busted.

I was awakened early one morning and marched into the still-dark living room for a thorough debriefing. Still bleary-eyed with zero idea that our foolproof plan had come unraveled, I struggled to understand the barrage of questions. *What was I thinking? Didn't I know how many crazy people were kidnapping girls on bicycles?* At one point, I distinctly remember my mom saying, "You're showing your true colors." I was baffled, wondering if "true colors" meant there was some type of visible aura giving me away. (Cyndi Lauper cleared that up for me a few years later.)

Sock-drawer escape plans aside, I was a pretty well-behaved kid. I wasn't robbing banks or punching other kids in the face; I was just full of energy and questions . . . for authority. My mom says she relied heavily on the classic parenting book *The Strong-Willed Child*, which is chock-full of buzzwords like *defiant* and *stubborn* that described me to a T. Rather than blindly accepting the rules and norms as they existed, I wanted to know WHY. When the boundaries didn't make sense to me, I pushed them.

News traveled quickly to my mother if I caused even the slightest trouble in school, a fact made especially painful by another one of our house rules: "If you get paddled at school, you get paddled at home." If a teacher felt I'd earned it in the classroom, there was heck to pay at home.

I will go to my grave convinced that the buildup to the spanking at home was infinitely worse than the punishment itself. It usually started with my mom saying the most ominous sentence a parent can utter: "We'll talk about this when we get home." From there, it would morph into a lengthy bedroom discussion of what I'd done wrong, followed by an interminable period of time for me to "think about it" before Mom returned for the final sentencing. I am a people pleaser by nature, so everything about this scenario felt like a nightmare. Not only did I not want to provoke my mother's disapproval, I most certainly did not want to be given an extended period of time to internalize the nuances of it.

Despite the terror this routine set off in me, I refused to cry when spanked, mostly because I usually thought the punishment did not fit the crime. In school, at home, and at church, I was constantly getting in trouble because I couldn't—or wouldn't?—stop talking. Today, I make a good living doing just that, so I'd like to argue that it's all worked out fine.

What doesn't work out fine is having your mother as a substitute teacher in high school. In ninth grade, one of my favorite teachers went on extended medical leave, and my mom got hired to pick up the slack.

"Your mom's cool, right?" the reigning sophomore hunk asked me when our teacher broke the news.

"Uhhh, no," I stammered. Even back then, I knew the wisdom of managing expectations.

Trust me, the tension ratcheted up to another level when she showed up to class one day dressed as Madonna.

Days before, the superstar had graced the cover of *TIME* magazine. I distinctly remember discussing her celebrity status on our drive home from school and making the mistake of saying to my mom, "Wouldn't it be awesome to be her, just for one day!?" Mom was horrified, both by Madonna's general existence and by the fact that her daughter would aspire to be anything like her for ANY amount of time. Madonna was everything my parents disapproved of, wrapped up in a single celebrity package.

And so, to hammer home the most embarrassing object lesson in history, Mom spent the next day teaching my high school class as the Material Girl. I recall a lacy headband, lots of bracelets and eyeliner, and a lecture punctuated with an overdose of "like," "grody," and "fer sure." I can only thank God she didn't actually burst into a chorus of "Like a Virgin."

As much as I resented my mom's guerrilla campaign to keep me on the straight and narrow, even then I took comfort in the fact that she gave me the perfect out for the moral choices that face every high schooler. When presented with peer pressure or a somewhat questionable decision, I could always easily fall back on the excuse, "My mom would kill me." (I'm not even sure I was kidding.) But more than giving me an out, she also gave me a set of core principles that guide me to this day. They were deeply rooted in a faith that taught me that my Heavenly Father's acceptance was the only thing I really needed in life.

I remember my mom finding me crying in my bedroom one day after I'd been left out of something. I halfway expected her to give me a lecture about counting my blessings. Instead, she listened to my story and then promised that one day I would forget about this perceived slight. She's right: I can't tell you now what had me sobbing.

My mom taught me to respect myself, and to question anyone who would ask me to sacrifice my integrity. As boy crazy as I eventually got, Mom encouraged me to draw lines early and often. She told me how valuable I was, how nothing could separate me from God's love, and that God had someone just as amazing out there waiting for me. (There was heavy emphasis on the "waiting" part, since I wouldn't be allowed to date until I'd secured a PhD.)

It breaks my heart when I see young women swept up in today's celebrity culture that encourages them to give themselves away for the sake of a few likes on social media. It makes me wish that everyone had someone in their life to remind them, "You are worth more." Maybe having the world's meanest mom wasn't such a bad thing after all.

Footloose, But Not Fancy-Free

Growing up, my mom wasn't the only one keeping tabs on my shenanigans. She had plenty of assistance from our church and school community, which operated a lot like the town from the box office hit *Footloose*. Our school had chapel speakers who explained how secular music was filled with diabolical messages that you could hear if you played the songs backward. School dances were never going to happen, and our cheerleading uniforms were modest to the point of invoking considerable mockery from opposing schools. (Trust me, they were calling us "Jesus freaks" long before the hit song made it a badge of honor.) School felt like a cozy, at times suffocating, cocoon—albeit one full of love and good intentions.

Trust me, though, even if my parents and our tight-knit circle had schemed to make me as uncool as possible—and I'm pretty sure they did—I didn't really need their help. While my friends were sneaking around trying to kiss boys, I was wearing Coke-bottle glasses, curling up with stacks of books, and nailing down Bible verses in hopes of winning the Sunday school Memory Challenge. (You know I did.) As a childhood birthday present one year, I requested tickets to the local dinner theater production of the musical *Oliver*. That about sums it up.

My love of musical theater was born out of a visit my family took to New York City when I was nine. We were accompanying my stepfather on a business trip, and I could not contain my excitement. Even the emergency landing we had to do in New Jersey was thrilling! This was the Big Apple circa 1980. Let's just say it had some rough edges. Streets coated with a layer of trash and cigarette butts, people dressed in clothes that I never imagined existed . . . you get the picture.

Never mind all that. This was the big time, and we were ready to shine. For the second night of our trip, we had secured tickets to the hit musical *Annie*. Having never seen a Broadway play but knowing that NYC was superfancy, Mom and I had packed long gowns to wear to the theater. Picture us walking the mean streets in floor-length velvet with ruffles. There was a chill in the air, and I remember asking my mom why so many women were barely wearing any clothes, and why they seemed so friendly toward the men on the street.

Imagine our shock when we arrived at the theater in our formal wear, only to see our fellow ticket holders decked out in their finest tracksuits and denim. Nine-year-old me felt sorry for them. "They must be so embarrassed," I whispered to my mom.

When we returned home, I knew my destiny was to find my way back to Broadway. We found a copy of the *Annie* score at my local music store, and morning, noon, and night

I banged out those tunes on our trusty upright while singing at the top of my lungs. I don't remember my parents objecting. They seemed happy to have their hyperactive child occupied, even if they never once requested an encore.

As much as I loved music, dancing had always been forbidden. In my family's social circle, the activity was considered too dangerous for young people with raging hormones. My cool older cousins, on the other hand, took every dance lesson imaginable, and I was totally psyched to attend all their recitals without exception. From the sequin-encrusted costumes to the rock music that blared from the speakers, it was my one permitted brush with the wild side—a place I could visit twice a year for those shows. When Halloween rolled around, if I wasn't already dressing up like an Old Testament character, I would squeal with delight as the girls let me pick through their old costumes for something to wear.

My parents always warned me about the dangers of peer pressure, but it's easy to ignore peer pressure when you don't have many peers. At school, I was always the nerd—partly because I started school a year early and tagged along with my classmates like a little sister. I couldn't date or drive until long after my classmates fulfilled those rites of passage. Before cell phones came along, I could only chat on the phone in the white-hot spotlight of our mustard yellow kitchen. Calling boys was completely forbidden. (Mom was a Rules Girl long before the book came out.) And if they did call? No whispering, and no conversations longer than twenty minutes. I wore handmade clothes, had glasses, and adored school and Jesus. Other kids made me feel awkward. (Maybe that's why I talked my way into joining our church's adult choir when I was in seventh grade, officially cementing my status as a Junior Church Lady.)

I always had the underlying awareness that I was not cool, but one particular sucker punch came in eighth grade when our family moved to Tallahassee, hundreds of miles away from the friends I'd known since pre-K. I spent much of that school year sitting alone at lunch and desperately trying to impress the popular kids by peppering conversations with references to TV shows and hit songs that I knew little about. I spent hours scouring the mall for final markdowns in an effort to whip my homespun wardrobe into shape. In sum, I tried way too hard, which to the actual cool kids only telegraphed one message: desperation.

I thought my efforts had finally won them over when an announcement came, saying I had been voted the class representative to the Valentine's Sweetheart Court. It truly wasn't until I stepped out onto the basketball court for the halftime ceremony and my classmates erupted in cackles that I realized they'd voted for me as a joke. I held my head up, but I felt like dying on the inside. These kids hadn't accepted me. I was a certified loser.

At moments, though, I saw there was a point in the way my parents raised me, and the person I was becoming. In middle school, I remember feeling like I'd have to stop showing up for class if I didn't buy a Members Only jacket. Our family didn't have money in the budget for trendy items. Mom usually procured hand-me-downs from my cousins and then worked her magic at the sewing machine. We grew and canned our own produce, clipped coupons, and always made sure we helped those less fortunate than us.

I got a modest allowance for doing chores around the house, so I saved and saved to secure my entry to the Members Only club. But by the time I came up with the cash, I realized I didn't value the jacket as much as I thought I would. All of a sudden, I felt protective of the money I'd worked so hard to scrape together. I discovered what my parents were always trying to teach me: self-discipline pays off.

My childhood is one that many people can't comprehend, especially in today's permissive society. But it made me exactly who I am. Curfews, rules, embarrassing parental displays—they all kept me from making mistakes I couldn't undo. As a teenager, I resented being held to totally different standards than my peers, but now I understand where my parents were coming from. They weren't raising my friends. They were raising me.

To this day, my mom will say, "Tell me about all the bad things you did back in high school!" She always seems disappointed when I explain that my adolescent treachery extended no further than making prank calls from the bowling alley where she and my stepdad played in the Friday-night church league while I chased new high scores on Ms. Pac-Man. (College, though? There may be a few PG-rated adventures she still doesn't know about . . .)

That feeling of being on the edge of being accepted by the cool kids—but not quite—has always stayed with me. I think it's why I love covering stories about underdogs and people who are quirky. I gravitate to the person at the party who looks like they feel even more out of place than I do. Often, this turns out to be the most elderly guest. Who has better stories and advice than someone who's been on this planet for decades longer than the rest of us?

My mom has always taken outsiders under her wing, with gusto. I can't count the number of times we had Sunday dinner or a holiday meal with a stranger seated at the table. Mom would run to Publix for a few more sticks of butter—this is the South we're talking about, after all—and come back with a heretofore unknown individual who had nowhere to go. Presto! For all Mom knew, they could've been a long-lost cousin or a fugitive from the law, but in our house they became the guest of honor. I often had to stop midmeal and ask, "Could you pass the rolls, and, um . . . what's your name again?"

It was a strange family quirk, but my parents did it because they believed what Christ said when he talked about feeding the hungry and inviting in strangers. "Truly I tell you, whatever you did for one of the least of these brothers and sisters of mine, you did for me."

That doesn't mean my mom's generosity doesn't also give me ulcers. Years ago I called her up to chat about what she had going on that day. She went on excitedly about her newest friend and her plans to deliver that friend a meal.

"Oh, where does she live?" I asked.

After an uncharacteristic pause, Mom replied, "Um, *he* lives in the woods behind . . ."

"MOM! No! I forbid this!" I said. But she was undeterred. She's always convinced that Jesus—and at times, a firearm—will get her home safely. So far, they have.

Keeping It Clean

My wonderful stepdad, who came into our lives when I was just a toddler and taught me everything from bike riding to squirrel hunting, has the cleanest guns in America. That's because he was always cleaning them when my dates came to pick me up.

Keep in mind I wasn't allowed to date until my senior year, long after shedding my giant glasses and braces. Even then, there was none of the "I'll honk and you just run out to the car" business on Roxbury Avenue in Tallahassee. Nope. My dates underwent a background check that even the FBI would've thought excessive: a chat with the boy's parents, a full vetting of all his friends and associates, and an exceptionally stern lecture about what time I was expected home. Needless to say, I didn't go on many dates.

When I really think about it, my stepdad's rules may have been where my love of storytelling began. You see, I truly was never up to trouble—at least not much of it—but I may have had to spin a yarn or two simply to be able to go out with my friends for noncriminal endeavors, like hanging out at McDonald's after youth group. "Shannon, you know you're not allowed to ride with teen drivers," my stepdad would say. "I know, but that guy *looks* twenty, right??" I would counter. (I'm not sure why I thought that one would work . . .)

During my senior year, though, my pristine reputation took a hit when our principal found me caught in the middle of a minor scandal. After being passed over twice, I had joined a girls' civic club whose initiation process included some relatively mild hazing rituals. That year, the initiation involved dragging the new members straight out of bed, putting them on the hoods of our cars, and slowly driving them through the grounds of our rival school in their PJs. We did the deed and thought we made a clean getaway, but several students who saw us in action apparently went straight to their headmaster.

I knew there was trouble when we all got called in to see the principal later that day. After outlining the charges against us and relaying the less-than-cordial call he had received from his counterpart at the rival school, the principal asked everyone who was not involved to leave the room. I didn't move. He looked straight at me and tried again, "I said—everyone who was NOT involved can leave." I was paralyzed. By the look on his face, so was he.

My dad wasn't a daily physical presence in my life, but he stayed deeply involved in my upbringing even after the divorce. He and Mom never spoke ill of each other in my presence. They sat together at graduations, awards ceremonies, and other rites of passage, making the best of an unusual arrangement after my stepparents came along. The men laughingly called each other "husband-in-law." I'm sure it helped that the one parenting principle they all agreed on was a healthy dose of discipline. Detours into things like PJ-gate would not go over well. That's why I never told them about it!

My dad, a law enforcement officer and Marine, was a straight shooter. If we kids slept in to some slothlike hour during our stays with him—you know, like 8:00 a.m.—he'd bellow, "They've already had lunch at Parris Island; let's go!" (He loved referencing the Marine boot camp that he says turned him "into a man.") There were no excuses and no crying. Study hard, commit, and follow through.

Mom and Dad were unified in their goal to get me as much education and opportunity as possible. They knew what I was capable of, so if a "B" showed up on my report card, the restrictions immediately kicked in—along with plenty of support.

But as much as they pushed me to succeed, there was also a constant drumbeat about staying humble. My mom often quoted Philippians 2:3, "Let nothing be done through strife or vainglory; but in lowliness of mind let each esteem others better than themselves." It sounds so simple and inspirational in theory, but in real life it takes some doing.

Like many kids, I attempted all kinds of hobbies before finally finding one for which I had at least some functional affinity. First came my ill-fated foray into gymnastics at age five. Hot off the 1976 Summer Olympics, like thousands of little girls around the globe, I begged my parents to take a class. My instructor sized me up very quickly—and accurately, I might add, since in this sport that favors the small,

I was already as tall as her. By the end of the multiweek course, it also became clear that I had zero flexibility and skills. I couldn't touch my toes or pull off a basic cartwheel, a fact that hasn't changed to this day.

Despite these setbacks, as our "graduation" ceremony approached, I was already begging my parents to sign me up for the next level.

"I'm so excited," I squealed, "but what if I don't get picked?"

"Honey, everyone gets invited to the next class," my mom assured me, knowing that the organization only makes money if kids keep enrolling. But guess who didn't get promoted to the next level? Yep. Even as a five-year-old, I was such a gymnastics failure that the school felt bad taking my parents' money! Mom didn't sugarcoat it. It was time to move on.

I enjoyed more success during my brief career as an elementary school majorette. I loved the biweekly practices, where we learned how to march in formation and twirl batons like pros. Our instructor even told us we would get to march in a parade at the end! We fund-raised to pay for our jazzy costumes, but the real excitement came when our instructor showed us batons that could be outfitted with a glow stick on each end. I couldn't believe my eyes. Glittering AND glowing? Must. Have.

The instructor explained that if we wanted to get our hands on those glowy things, we'd need to do a second round of fund-raising. This time we collected newspapers and turned them in for recycling. I'm not sure who, but someone was paying us by the pound. I bugged our neighbors every day and got superpumped when the mother lode dropped on Sundays. Long after fulfilling my personal quota, I kept on collecting because *darnit*, everyone in our troupe deserved to glow with the best of them.

On the day of the parade, the dozen or so of us lined up shimmering and strutting, perfecting our moves as we prepared to wow the crowds. It was the moment of truth. As the instructor attached the glow sticks one by one to our glimmering silver batons, my mom urged me to wait my turn. Then, suddenly, there were none left.

Tears were about to flow. Not mine, mind you. I had brought in far more than my share of papers and I was ready to GLOW! Someone else who hadn't pulled their newspaper-collecting weight would have to give me theirs.

But before I could stomp off and deliver a dose of glittery justice, Mom pulled me aside. "Remember, many of these girls have less than we do. We have plenty of blessings, so let's be a blessing to someone else."

Mom was right. I wasn't happy about it, but I got the message.

It's a lesson that's served me well over the years, even if I haven't always managed to live it. I believe most of us are primarily somewhat selfish by default, and how much we work to overcome that impulse is a personal choice. Luckily, I've always had backup on that front. It's a task that no one can do on their own, so I pray daily to become more like Christ and less like the world. Or, failing that, at least more like my mom.

Even now, when I look into the camera and prepare to go live, I have a mantra: *humbly grateful*. Anything and everything entrusted to me on this earth is simply mine to manage while I'm here, including my stepdad's very shiny gun collection.

Give Me Liberty

Selecting a college has become a multiyear, multivisit odyssey that begins before kids lose their braces. That was most definitely not the case when I was growing up. In my parents' house, there were no visits to far-flung campuses or hours spent poring over countless brochures. (For the millennials among you: brochures were these preinternet pieces of paper that extolled the virtues of each educational institution.) Both my parents had attended Florida State University, and as a high school senior already living in Tallahassee, I was fortunate to be awarded an academic scholarship that virtually covered the full cost of my four-year undergraduate degree.

My parents were big proponents of higher education, but it never occurred to them that me winding up with an Ivy League degree would get me any further in life than a degree from a state school. In reality, my dad was no fan of "fancy pants" people who were "educated beyond their intelligence." Other than Florida State, I only remember applying to one other school: Liberty University.

I'd been to a cheer camp and competition on Liberty's campus, and a couple of my older friends had been recruited to play sports there, so I was getting plenty of scoop on the Christian college in Virginia. My parents, not surprisingly, had laid down the law: "The only way you're going away to college is if it's a religious institution with a curfew and LOTS of parental involvement." Attending Liberty would be exponentially more expensive for my family, but they left the decision to me and never hinted that I should choose a college based on the financial burden. As graduation approached, I still hadn't made up my mind about the long-term plan, so I started summer classes at Florida State and planned to use that time to make a decision about the fall.

Attending a massive university was nothing like the cozy cocoon of my small Christian high school. A friend of mine played football for Florida State at the time, and I remember feeling semicool (only momentarily) when he introduced me and my friends to some of the players. I was spreading my wings a bit, but still unsure whether I should stay at FSU or move to Liberty after the summer. Then I walked into my psychology class.

It was a typical freshman class, large and unruly. I'd never met an academic challenge that couldn't be overcome through my tried-and-true study habits, but this time a new obstacle showed up in my way. From the moment when I turned in my first project, it became clear that my personal beliefs were going to be seen as illegitimate and flawed.

I don't remember the exact wording of that assignment, but it had something to do with writing about the most important thing in our lives. I chose to focus on my faith, how seeking God's approval would always be my compass and my main priority. Upon reading the essay, my professor chose to level a withering critique about being in love with a boyfriend who didn't exist. When I went to her office to discuss it with her, she looked at me with what felt like a mix of pity and amusement. "You'll grow out of it," she said.

I was well equipped to stand on principle, but at seventeen I wasn't sure I wanted to go into full-on battle mode in my first experience with a secular learning environment. Did I really want to put up with this for the next four years?

By the end of the summer I had decided Liberty was the best place for me. I wanted to spend more time putting down my spiritual and intellectual roots while enjoying my college experience. My parents backed the decision, and Mom and I loaded up to make the trip with my friend Mark and his mother, Amy. The drive took at least twelve hours, snaking through Atlanta's agonizing traffic and the two Carolinas, but Mark and I were so excited to get there that it seemed to last for days. Mom was tearful as she dropped me off and said good-bye, though I wouldn't have blamed her for being relieved after all my minor teenage rebellions. I was already champing at the bit to get moved in.

These were no luxury accommodations, just two sets of bunk beds, two small closets, and four girls from around the country. Our room had a phone, but it only worked for numbers on campus, and all other calls had to be made from the single pay phone out in the hall. The hallway phone was always in use, so it took a couple of weeks for me to call my mom and tell her how I was doing. "Don't you *hi* me!" she said when I finally rang home. "I've been worried sick for days!" She had spent the last two weeks convinced I'd joined a traveling circus or had eloped with the first boy I met.

I thrived at Liberty. It was full of kids who had hopes and dreams, who loved life and saw the world through a different lens. It took years before I realized just how different our campus was from the vast majority of collegiate experiences. There was a curfew, enforced by a guard stationed at the entrance/exit to campus. If you showed up to the booth one minute late, you'd be stopped, and you better have a legitimate excuse. Penalties incurred demerits. If you racked up enough of those, you'd be booted from campus.

You could also pick up demerits for having a messy room, skipping chapel services, hair too long on the boys and skirts too short for the girls. That last one was the only one that ever seemed to get me into trouble, but even that was rare. I was so well behaved on campus, following the rulebook to a T, that I was eventually asked to be a student member of the Review Board. We handled the cases of students facing expulsion, and they came to us as a last appeal. Being seen as a "goody-goody" was fine with me. People assumed I wouldn't be sneaking out, drinking, or sleeping around. They were right, and it saved me a lot of trouble in college. (Even if it did leave me mortified when I found out one of my friends beat curfew by sneaking back to campus in the trunk of someone's car.)

Liberty felt like a gigantic version of the smaller Christian school I'd attended since preschool, but that didn't mean it was without its setbacks—especially once I started dating. A long-term high school boyfriend had broken my heart by ending things before we went off to our separate colleges. Here I was now, on a campus with thousands of new faces. At first, I was determined to play the field, but the resolution ended quickly when I fell for a handsome sophomore from South Carolina. I'll never forget how it stung when I overheard a friend of his, who was part of the in-crowd, say, "You could do so much better than her."

I've faced comments like that throughout my life. For the most part, having someone tell me I'm not good enough is just gasoline on my fire. In many ways I feel like I've sort of made a cottage industry out of being underestimated. College was no exception.

I pushed hard to get a 4.0 my first semester, yet there was a fair amount of eye rolling from my parents when I announced that I wanted to major in accounting. After watching me force the neighbor girls to take part in my amateur, yet elaborate, musical productions as a girl—with me in the starring role, of course—let's just say my parents were rather skeptical that I'd enjoy a life of numbers. After spending my entire Thanksgiving break poring over spreadsheets to find a missing thirty cents, I decided they were right.

Next up? Political science. When I announced the new direction, everyone's first question was, "What are you going to do with that?" Who knows, but I knew I had a passion for politics. I loved the coursework and loved spending hours debating the finer points of parliamentary procedure in the student senate, but as the semesters stretched on, I did start to wonder what I'd do with that degree. It seemed all the other poli sci majors were planning to teach or go to grad school. At that point, I wasn't interested in either.

I finally settled on a business degree with a focus on management. It felt like a good base that would offer me more postgraduation options. I became fascinated by the study of what motivates human beings in the workplace and beyond. The studies gave me an interesting window into people I found to be so different from me. I always assume people have ulterior motives—Lord knows I do!—so I like being able to get to the crux of what's driving them. Some people want money, and others fight for relevance or public acclaim. But nearly everyone's after something.

The further I got into my coursework, the more our professors assigned us group projects. My partners either thought I was their best friend or worst nightmare, because I basically did all the work. At that point in my life, doing it any other way would have stressed me beyond my limits, because I didn't trust anyone else not to ruin my grade with their lack of commitment to the project. By my senior year, that strategy wore me out to the point where I basically checked out from a semester-long project in which our group was supposed to run an imaginary airline. (Thanks, Seth, for saving us all on that one.)

At first, I chose my friends and my endeavors very carefully, afraid to enroll in classes or activities where success wasn't guaranteed. But college is for putting yourself in situations that will stretch you. It wasn't until later in college that I started to dip my toe into experiences that would challenge me, or sometimes even make me uncomfortable. One of the greatest adventures I had was a trip to Brazil.

I had always wanted to go on a mission trip during my years at Liberty, and an opportunity finally came the summer before my senior year. Each year we sent teams to work with already-established missionaries with whatever needs they had on the ground, and this year they were sending a team to Brazil. Even though my family wasn't wealthy, I'd always been told that simply by growing up in America I had a much easier life than billions of people around the world. I was ready to confront that in a personal way.

Once I committed to a few weeks in Brazil, I started fund-raising to help cover the mission. People were generous, but I still had a gap with the deadline approaching. I felt the Lord tugging at me to use a chunk of my savings to finish financing the trip. I was a struggling college kid, but I've never regretted the decision.

Once we got to Brazil, our team would set up on the streets and perform, work in schools and orphanages—even visit a notorious prison. Some students were trained to put on puppet shows for kids, others to perform gymnastics routines. I ended up being assigned to a singing group, with the nerve-racking task of learning all our songs in Portuguese in a span of eight weeks. I'm not the world's greatest singer, and at that point I knew a grand total of zero words in the language we'd be singing.

Two fellow students of ours had grown up in Brazil, so they stopped by some of our rehearsals and even made phonetic recordings of all the songs. All semester long, that cassette was in my Walkman nonstop. (See, Mom, Jesus found a use for that Walkman, after all!) Trying to manage the months of preparation along with a heavy class load felt crushing at times, but we got it done.

The trip changed my world perspective almost immediately. We went to places with no electricity, with farm animals running through the shacks where large families lived happily. The people of Brazil were effusively warm and welcoming. They even remarked on how stiff the Americans seemed! They watched a lot of television from the United States, including a heavy rotation of *Dallas* and *Dynasty* reruns, which led them to assume that we all lived in mansions and ate dinner wearing evening gowns. I was struck by how joyous and giving everyone was, even in the places with the most devastating poverty.

Those weeks were a reality check, showing me just how much of a spoiled brat I was. But they were full of laughs, too—many at my own expense. During one of our first performances, I belted out the only solo lines I had in the show—something about God being mighty. The audience gasped, and then seemed to break into nervous laughter. Immediately after the show, one of our translators informed me that my pronunciation was so garbled that I was essentially singing about God passing gas. I felt mortified and spent the rest of the trip listening to that worn-out cassette until my batteries eventually died.

All month we stayed in modest accommodations in varying states of upkeep. I can still see one of the showers like it was yesterday. Fortunately, the place had running water, but we were in and out of the shower in record speed. First, because the water was freezing and, second, because of the squirrel-sized spiders hanging around in there.

And then there was the morning when I woke up to urgent banging on my door. I threw the door open to see that one of the other young women on the trip had brought a very unique problem upon herself. She had burned her bangs off with an overheated curling iron, singeing them down to the roots. Tears ran down her face as I tried to help her style the remaining hair in a flattering do, but we all learned a big lesson. If you don't have the correct adapter, don't jam your US appliances into the wall socket.

That trip took me on an adventure I never could have predicted, just one of the many ways I learned to take risks and stretch myself during those years. What I didn't know at that point in my life was that a poster I spotted on campus would lead me on an even crazier roller coaster.

"Don't Let This Be the Most Exciting Thing"

Like many little girls who grew up in the 1970s and 1980s, I gathered around the TV once a year with my mom, and often my grandmother, to watch the Miss America Pageant. We all marveled at these women who seemed like creatures from another planet, studded with sequins and full of ideas for saving the world. The whole thing seemed so sparkly and glamorous. Each year I would watch with increased interest, trying to discern what exactly caused the winners to stand out from the other contestants.

These years were the heyday of the VCR, so I began by making sure I had one of those chunky tapes fed into the electronic beast and went through the fifteen-step recording process (checking and rechecking, because there was that heartbreaking time when a critical episode of *Dallas* didn't record as planned). In those days there was no replay, no looking on the web for whatever your truculent VCR had decided not to record.

I watched those tapes over and over, looking for the winning formula. I studied facial expressions, walks, makeup, shoes, gowns, and even what nail polish the contestants were wearing. I figured there must be some code to be cracked—that if I could figure out what made these women seem so polished, maybe I could follow the same steps and execute my own extreme makeover.

Years later, as I was walking across Liberty's campus, I stopped in my tracks when I spotted a beautiful poster inviting interested students to attend a meeting about the Miss Lynchburg Pageant. The local competition served as a feeder for Miss Virginia and Miss America contests and was known for attracting top competitors. I had seen the same poster my freshman year, but I was too chicken to even attend the informational meeting. This time, I knew I had to do it.

Even as I jotted down the information, my stomach was doing somersaults. I had done a couple of high school pageants (in borrowed dresses) where the judging focused on academics and community service, but nothing close to this scale. Besides, I was nothing like the young women I had seen on TV, with their perfect bodies and eloquent answers about world affairs. Who was I to think that I could glide across the stage with poise and confidence? Just the cost of a single evening gown was far beyond my imagination.

I remember going to that initial workshop and getting the distinct impression that no one understood why I was there. I had mousy hair, amateur makeup, and frumpy clothes. Many of the other competitors had competed at the state level before, and some had even finished as runners-up to Miss Virginia. Their experience showed, from their flawless talent performances to their stunning wardrobes. I was way out of my league. When the organizers asked the contestants to run through our talent routines, they wrapped up before they even got to me. "Um, I didn't go yet," I quietly pointed out. "I'm going to play the piano." I felt invisible. Still, I was determined to give it a shot.

In the whirlwind of preparations, I picked up some information about a stylist named Garry Viar who had helped many of the successful candidates. His ageless face, cowboy boots, and sunny smile could make a believer out of anyone—and it usually started with him working some hair magic. At some point in high school, the sunny blond hair of my youth had morphed into a shade that a high school rival once dubbed "dishwater blond." I remember turning around in the chair once Garry had done his thing . . . and almost immediately bursting into tears. Even a few subtle highlights felt radical to me then.

I rushed out of the salon to give a presentation for one of my classes. Running across campus, I was convinced everyone was laughing at my ridiculous makeover. I felt like every eye was trained on me, and I just wanted to hide. Very quickly, though, the rave reviews started to roll in. Many of the girls wanted to know where this glistening new mane of mine had come from. I was stunned, but it made me realize that these pageant folks may actually have known what they were doing.

I dove into my Miss Lynchburg preparation with gusto. Over the Christmas break at home in Florida my mom and I bought an evening gown at a bridal salon, and I borrowed many of the other things I would need. (The jewelry alone would've cost more than an entire year of textbooks.) I searched out every way I could find to get access to a piano on campus to practice one of my favorite church solos. Little did I know, the experienced competitors spent the same window of time meeting with professional coaches, ordering custom wardrobes, and drilling through practice interviews. To say I was a novice is a gross understatement.

Leading up to the day of competition, my mom and I had heard about a sticky substance that the pros used to keep their swimsuits from riding up. One of the more decorated veterans told me it was the same stuff athletes used to get a good grip on the ball. "You can find it at any sporting goods store," she said.

As we scrambled to pull together all the last-minute details, my mom ran out to get the sticky stuff and I hustled to the auditorium to prep for the big night. After all those years of watching from afar, I was excited to think I'd scored one of the insiders' secrets!

The opening rounds went by in a blur, and suddenly it was time for the swimsuit competition. As I lifted my pristine suit backstage, Mom began spraying and then gasped. "There's something wrong, honey. Don't let go of that suit!" Turns out, the spray came in different colors, and a thick brown sludge had just been sprayed on my backside.

I couldn't let go of the white swimsuit, but it was imperative that we start scrubbing that brown goo off and get on stage *stat*. A couple of girls helped me try, but the clock was ticking. I wound up walking onstage with bright red cheeks (both sets) and a bright white swimsuit with some brown stains on the seat. But that wasn't even the worst thing that happened to me on the stage that night.

Despite having played the piano for years, I had never

gotten over the nerves of performing for a live audience. I think *terrified* would be the appropriate word to describe the feeling I had onstage, especially when playing from memory like I was on that night. As I took my seat and adjusted the bench, I rehearsed the song over and over in my head. My fingers were shaking, but I took a deep breath and dove in.

Then, all my worst fears materialized. Halfway through the piece, my memory went completely blank. I could feel myself careening toward disaster. My fingers lost their way, and the piece came to a complete stop.

An awkward silence settled over the room. As I looked out into the dark auditorium and saw the audience staring back in shock and pity, I felt like dying of a heart attack right there on the spot. All I could think about was how my parents had traveled all the way from Florida to support me, and what a waste that turned out to be. After what seemed like an eternity, I somehow picked up the piece and stumbled my way through the end.

With the audience applauding politely, I ran off the stage and collapsed into embarrassed sobs. The tears stung as they ran down my cheeks, turning my makeup into a ruined piece of abstract art.

Somehow I pulled myself together for the evening gown competition and final question. The latter had always been my comfort zone. No matter the question, what the judges are looking for is confidence and the ability to articulate a point of view. I knew my gown didn't stand up to the glittering, sophisticated creations my competitors were wearing, but I never doubted my capacity to speak my mind.

The interview portions made up such a large portion of the scoring that I still managed to finish third runner-up by the end of the night. But as I left the stage, I just wanted to pretend the whole thing had never happened.

As I walked into an informal after-party, I heard one of the more experienced girls talking about me. "I can't believe she did better than me!" she said. "Her evening gown looked like a wedding dress. It was hideous." I was too far into the room to back out and pretend I hadn't heard her. Talk about awkward.

I spotted my parents and fell into my mom's comforting hug. "Sweetie, you gave it your best shot," she said softly. "But maybe Miss America isn't your thing."

Most everyone else agreed, including me. But as we debriefed over the next week, there was one notable exception to that opinion: Garry Viar. "You know you're going to Miss America one day," he said when he heard I was considering early retirement.

"What are you talking about?!" I said. "You saw that disaster!" I'm pretty sure I looked at him like he'd just stepped off a spaceship.

But Garry said I had more potential than just about any contestant he'd ever worked with, and he was determined to make me believe it too. He was the director of another local pageant that took place in just another month. He convinced me to sign up. If I didn't dive back in right away, he said, I might never try again.

So I decided to give it another shot. I found new places I could practice the piano and rented upscale pageant clothing from more experienced contestants. My parents weren't there when I took to the stage for the Miss Amherst County Pageant, but they were the first ones I called after I won. This was before cell phones, so I remember asking the restaurant where the after-party was held if I could use their phone to call home collect. I could tell my parents were shocked, but it was real: we were headed to the Miss Virginia Pageant.

The thought of performing for competition at that level, with a live TV audience and thousands more watching in the theater, was almost too much for my stomach. But I was in excellent hands. Garry went above and beyond to build my confidence. He constantly reinforced his belief that I was going to succeed, scheduled meetings with experts, and kept an eye out for the perfect gown.

I took fitness classes at a studio below Garry's salon. The quirky, high-energy instructor ran us all over the place, right past the startled patrons getting their hair cut and colored. I started working on a challenging classical piece that my beloved high school piano teacher selected, having competed in the Miss America system herself. Then there was the business of putting together a vast enough wardrobe to get me through a full week of competition and public events associated with the state pageant. We got some sponsors to cover some of the casual wear, but the formal gowns were beyond anything my family could have afforded at that point. Thanks to the enormous generosity of Garry and the Miss Amherst County Pageant, we never had to worry about that.

During those months of preparation, I often drove past a simple house in Lynchburg that had a small sign tacked to one of the trees in the yard. It said simply, MATTHEW 6:33. The verse says to seek first the kingdom of God and his righteousness, and God will take care of the rest. In the midst of all the work I was doing, that verse was a daily reminder to keep my eyes on the real prize.

I was morphing into the kind of confident young woman I'd seen on those Miss America stages as a kid. Like them, I had realized that it was okay to be a flawed human being simply working to be the best version of yourself. I had no idea where this journey was going to end, but every day it was stretching me and pushing me to achieve things I hadn't previously thought possible.

My goal was to make the top ten at Miss Virginia, which felt like a respectable showing for a first-year competitor. But Garry wouldn't let me settle. "You're going to win," he said, "and you better start believing that." Everywhere we went, he introduced me as "the next Miss Virginia." He even gave me motivational tapes with upbeat stories and subliminal messages like, "You're a winner! Yes, you!" I'm not going to lie—it was a little embarrassing. I couldn't tell whether Garry believed the things he was saying, or was just trying to build up a desperately insecure nineteen-year-old.

As we inched toward the state competition, I continued to struggle with enormous stage fright. It never hit me when I was answering a question—I've always been comfortable running my mouth—but the Chopin piece I'd picked for the talent portion haunted me day and night. A somber, highly technical piece, historians believe Chopin composed it in his grief over Poland's failed uprising against the Russian Empire in 1831. It pushed the limits of my skills and required endless hours of practice. People offered to get me some medication that would calm my nerves, but I felt in my heart that this would be a cop-out. The fear felt like a test of my faith, and I was convinced the Lord wanted me to rely fully on Him.

So I put in the hard work and plowed forward. During the nights of preliminary competition, everyone has a chance to compete in swimsuit, talent, and evening gown before the finalists are chosen. Those scores, combined with the judges' interview, decided the top ten. On the night I was set to perform my piano solo for the first time I became frantic. I had assumed I could see my mom and pray together before the performance, but the schedule wouldn't permit that. So after an emotional phone call and the most fervent prayer of my life, I turned to my Bible and asked the Lord to give me some guidance. I randomly opened to Psalm 34, and my heart leapt when I read verse 4: "I sought the Lord and he heard me and delivered me from all my fears." Since that day I've lost count of the tough moments when those words have come back to mind.

There's plenty of chatter surrounding pageant week as the local directors, veteran pageant watchers, makeup artists, stylists, and media speculate over who might win. But all week long, none of the speculation was about me—the green nineteen-year-old no one had ever heard of. I didn't win any of the preliminary awards and went into the final night hoping for the best. My supportive family was in the audience, along with those ubiquitous giant camcorders that parents used to tote around on their shoulders.

When the opening number ends and the emcee introduces

each contestant, the nerves really kick in. There's a buzz of nervous energy as each young woman takes her spot onstage to await the announcement of the ten finalists. For those who make it, the competition starts all over again. The nonfinalists are done for the night and left to consider whether they want to give it another shot next year. One after another the names were called, and my hopes of making the cut were fading. Then, just as my thoughts drifted to the question of whether I'd try again in the future, the announcer thundered: "Our ninth finalist, from Amherst County, Shannon Noelle DePuy."

Wow, this is really happening! I thought. Having achieved enough to not embarrass my family or Garry, I relaxed and started to enjoy the evening. Swimsuit competition went off without a hitch, and then it was time for what I feared most: the piano solo. I prayed my way through every note, and relief flooded over me when it was done.

Then came the reality check: the announcement of who won. This is an odd part of the pageant process. Most contestants want a respectable showing, but you don't want to finish so close to winning that there's a ton of pressure on you to perform the next year. Top ten is great. You're on the board, but you're flying under the radar. Once you ascend into the ranks of runner-up, though, everyone knows a target will be on your back when you compete the following year.

As the evening came to a close, I was very emotional. We all were. The competition is exhausting in every possible way—and I'm sure we were all starving, too. A couple of close friends had also made the finals, and I was silently cheering for one of them to take the crown. One by one, though, as the runners-up were announced, I began to feel real confusion about who would win. I thought the very best contenders had already been called out. And then, out of nowhere, a semitruck hit me. "Your new Miss Virginia: Miss Amherst County, Shannon Noelle DePuy!"

WHAT?!!? I immediately burst into tears and stumbled across the stage. The audience sprang to their feet, and the traditional Miss Virginia serenade music played. Suddenly a crown was on my head, roses were in my hands, and I was waving to the cheering crowd as I desperately tried to make eye contact with my family.

The organizers had made us all rehearse where to go and what to do when you win, but no one wants to pay attention because you don't want to seem like you *actually* think you're going to be taking that walk. Trust me, NO ONE was more stunned than me at that moment. I had never once let that vision enter my mind. As reality set in, I suddenly felt completely unprepared and terrified. I had planned to compete for two or three years before having a real shot at getting to Miss America, but now I was heading to the big leagues.

I hugged my good friend and fellow competitor Jennifer in a death grip and choked into her ear, "I can't do this. I'm not ready."

She hugged me back and said, "God has a plan. Trust this." The rest was a blur.

In retrospect, it's entertaining to watch the VHS tape my father recorded that night. The shot is steady as the emcee reads the runners-up, but when they call my name, the visual jumps all over the place—wildly swinging up and down and side to side—as my dad must have been hooting and hollering!

I was a swirl of emotions, a little girl whose grown-up dream was coming true ahead of schedule. I'd always believed in God's timing, but I felt like I was boarding a rocket ship without completing astronaut training. On the outside I looked just like the women I'd watched on-screen so many times: polished, glittering, and confident. I'd been pushed out of the nest, and now it was time to learn to fly.

With only a handful of weeks to prepare for Miss America, I was in shock. There were dozens of wardrobe decisions to make, a new piano instructor to hire, and travel arrangements and a jam-packed schedule of appearances at local parades, county fairs, and military bases to manage. It broke my heart to withdraw from Liberty for what would have been my junior year, but I'd just been drafted into a rather demanding full-time job.

Overwhelmed, that's how I felt. And not everyone was happy for me. The pageant world is notoriously gossipy, and plenty of people thought someone else should've won the state title. Thank goodness chat rooms and social media didn't exist then!

Thank goodness, too, that I wouldn't be alone. Every state titleholder has a traveling companion, or chaperone, an experienced woman who keeps you on schedule and oversees your travels. Mine went by the name Mean Momma Jean, or as we affectionately called her, MMJ. She'd been accompanying Miss Virginia for years and she didn't mince words. When it was time to get up early, when it was time to rehearse, when your gown got a little too snug—MMJ spoke the truth.

When I got to Miss America and met the other girls, they went on and on about how their chaperones ironed their clothes, did all the driving, made sure they got rest and had hot meals. That was not how it operated in Virginia. Momma Jean had a heart of gold, but a very stern exterior. She'd tell you if she thought you'd gained weight, didn't give your best speech, or missed a few notes on the keyboard. She was not there to coddle Miss Virginia. She was there to keep you in line and out of trouble. Oh, and she didn't have a driver's license, so I did all the driving.

When we finally arrived in Atlantic City, we were placed at Caesars Palace. Momma Jean enjoyed gambling and boxing, so she felt right at home on the Boardwalk. On one of our free afternoons, she and I were walking a few hotels down the strip to get an errand done when we saw a large entourage of people moving from store to store, closing each one down so some celebrity could shop in private. We nosed around and found out it was boxer Mike Tyson, who was on top of the world at the time.

I couldn't have cared less, but Momma Jean had a plan. "I've got Miss Virginia here with me and she's a big boxing fan," she said to one of Tyson's crew. "She'd love to say hello." With a head nod and a wave, we were ushered in with the group when Tyson took over the next store. I knew nothing about boxing, so I sat there awkwardly in my pink sweats without a stitch of makeup on, trying to make conversation. "So, Mr. Tyson, what's your life like?"

If we'd had cell phones back then, I could have snapped a quick picture of Momma Jean and Tyson and gotten the heck out of there. Instead, the pauses in conversation led to Tyson saying, "You? You're in the Miss America Pageant?" Trust me, Mr. Boxing Legend, I was just as stunned as you were! We eventually made a graceful exit and moved on.

The women at Miss America were phenomenal: future lawyers and doctors, teachers and scientists. The talents were varied, and their résumés eye-popping. They'd thought of everything this novice hadn't—like reserving the only piano in our hotel for rehearsal time. I was in over my head but couldn't turn back. Once you win a state title, you have one shot at Miss America. There's no do-over.

For weeks we pinged between public appearances, hours-long rehearsals, and traditional events like the annual parade down the Boardwalk. I remember one titleholder was so exhausted, she actually fell asleep atop her car halfway through the parade.

It took all I had to keep it together for my preliminary piano competition. I had prayed and asked God repeatedly to give me the confidence and skill to get through it. I got into the zone and headed to the stage determined to keep it together for the next five minutes. Then, as I took my seat on the bench, the emcee unexpectedly broke from the program and stopped to recognize a group of troops who were in the audience that night. I stood from the bench out of respect and began to clap. Someone remarked to me later what a "smart move" that was, but being smart had nothing to do with it. To me, it was a natural reaction. My family is filled with people who've served in every branch, and I'd grown up with a deep respect for our men and women in uniform.

I don't remember much more about that preliminary night, but I can recall with great detail the judges' interview—or rather, grilling—I went through that week. "There was a big KKK rally down South this week," the first question came. "Is that really what the First Amendment was intended to protect?" Before I could finish my answer, another judge jumped in. "People are dying of AIDS across the globe. Do you agree with the founder of your university, Jerry Falwell, that AIDS is a punishment on the gay community?" Fighting through the adrenaline, I spat out answers as we hit one topic after another, and then it was over.

I spotted one of my fellow contestants looking rather upset after her interview. When I tried to console her, she snapped, "I didn't come here to make friends! I came here to win!" (Turns out, she didn't do either.) It was a reality check: this was the big time.

As the final night approached, I was a tangle of emotions. Back then, communication with the outside world was nearly impossible on that final day. There were no cell phones, and we contestants had been sequestered at the performance hall from very early on in the day. Imagine how stunned I was, then, when an old-school telegram showed up for me just before we went on air. It was from my dorm parents and the girls on my hall back at Liberty. The message was short and sweet, but told me they were praying for me. No one was ever able to explain how that got through security, but it meant the world to me.

We started the live television show with our opening number and introductions. Backstage, the chaperones were being told in secret who had made the top ten, so they could start moving the finalists' gowns and costumes into a different section of the dressing area. Since we couldn't go back there, we were left in a holding space for several minutes through a series of commercials and the judges' introductions. The wait was excruciating. Each of us had spent weeks, months, and in some cases, years, preparing for this with the expectations of our families, our sponsors, and even our schools weighing heavily on us. One of the pageant staffers said, "Just think, if you get picked for the top ten you'll get to perform for eighty million people!" I wanted to run for the nearest exit.

Moments later I was shocked and then relieved to hear my name among the finalists. No matter what happened next, I would spend the next couple of hours living out my dream of competing in the Miss America Pageant. I'd done all the preparation I could months in advance. As long as I didn't fall—mission accomplished.

The piano was my one true challenge that night. Despite having poured myself into daily five-hour practices, I still couldn't disguise the fact that I'm no virtuoso. In fact, one newspaper said that my preliminary Chopin performance was "like watching someone pick through a minefield." But nothing was stopping me on the final night. My fate was in my Heavenly Father's hands, and I trusted that He hadn't brought me that far to fall apart. As I reached the final measures of the heavy piece I'd chosen, a huge smile broke out on my face. It didn't fit the tone of the piece, but it fit the victory I felt in overcoming my greatest fear. I left it all on the field that night.

Before long, the moment of truth arrived. The ten finalists lined the stage as, one by one, the women I'd thought had a real shot at the crown were called out for elimination. That left six of us, one of whom was about to have her life radically changed.

Suddenly, my mind flashed back to the time I'd spent as Miss Virginia, and I started crying. For the first time, I began praying that my name would NOT be called. Just a couple of years out of high school, I felt completely ill-equipped to face the national spotlight of becoming Miss America, knowing it would mean another year of piano solos and facing the media. The timing felt all wrong. I knew I had a lot more maturing to do before I was ready to step onto a national stage.

"Your new Miss America: Miss Illinois, Marjorie Judith Vincent!" More tears, but this time they represented my relief.

The next morning at breakfast, I could see that my dad was disappointed. Of course, he thought his daughter had been robbed. The competition had been a wild ride, and my dad had some words of caution before we left: "Don't let this be the most exciting thing that happens in your life." I was determined not to, but I still had a lot of work ahead. I would crisscross the historic, beautiful Commonwealth of Virginia for the next ten months before retiring for good from the world of pageantry . . . or so I thought.

Date Like a Man

Returning to campus at Liberty after my year as Miss Virginia was the best possible homecoming. My life had changed so much during the year away, but what hadn't changed was who I was at the core. Studying was still my happy place, and I was anxious to finish up my degree and figure out what was next. Thanks to my scholarship winnings from Miss America, the burden of tuition was all but erased for my final two years of school.

The peers I'd entered college with were now a year ahead of me academically and starting to look for jobs. The news wasn't good, and I could hear my dad's voice in my head: "Pick law school or medical school." The latter wasn't a realistic option for someone who nearly faints at the sight of a paper cut, but law school intrigued me. I started looking into it.

I also dove back into the dating game. After spending so much time in long-term relationships, I wasn't really sure how to see someone without immediately falling in love. But I have to say, if you're going to shop around, Liberty's a good place to do it. I met guys from all over the world on campus, and every last one of them treated me with respect. That doesn't mean it was easy. As a child of divorce, I wasn't sure I ever wanted to do the whole "white picket fence" thing. I was determined to make my own money and my own decisions, but that wasn't exactly the template some of the guys I dated were looking for, and those relationships fizzled. I did stupid things like fall for one best friend while I was dating the other one. I found it hard to hurt anyone, so I avoided difficult conversations about whether we truly connected or wanted the same things in life. I tried to make so many relationships work when it was obvious they wouldn't.

For me, a date wasn't just a date, and I didn't want to spend time with anyone I didn't think I might actually marry. Despite the jokes about "test-driving" a person like you would a car, I took it much more seriously. You trade cars in, sell them, or send them to the junkyard. I'm not doing that with a human being.

Before long, though, I was the one who got my heart broken. Really broken. I fell way too quickly for someone I didn't know well, and it ended in disaster. We've all been there. I rolled through every stop sign, ignored every red flag that the relationship wasn't a healthy one. I don't recommend this. It can feel like the most exciting roller-coaster ride in the world, but even those come to an abrupt halt at some point. For me, the end came when I found out he was seeing his teenage neighbor at the same time he was dating me "exclusively." (OUCH.) We all know couples who met and married within four months and lived happily ever after, but there's a reason those stories are the rare exception. Hats off to everyone who's experienced that needle-in-a-haystack miracle, but most of us need a lot more time to find the right person.

So, having sworn off men, I decided to date like one. I had one semester left at Liberty, and already knew I was heading home to go to law school. Nothing wrong with having dinner or seeing a movie with some cute guy, right? No emotional connections, though! Free stuff and fun—that's it. That's the lecture I gave myself. I meant it, but life had other plans in store.

For months, a friend of mine had been trying to introduce me to a handsome guy on campus. We didn't really run in the same circles, but it was hard to miss the tall, handsome baseball player with sparkling blue eyes. He seemed fun to be around, but I knew all about *those athletes*. Now would be the time to date him, though, because I was embarking on my "no strings attached, don't go on a date with anyone you'd actually fall in love with" phase. His name was Sheldon Bream. A friend had insisted that we meet at the Homecoming game the previous fall, even though we were both dating other people at the time. "He's here at the game, you're here—it's time to connect!" As I stood with my stepfather, she led Sheldon over and I was struck by just how handsome he was up close. We had a few friendly phone chats, but nothing more.

Sheldon's version of events is slightly different. Unbeknownst to me, after meeting at that Homecoming game, Sheldon went to his long-term girlfriend's house and broke up with her. As callous as that might sound, he says he was trying to do the honorable thing. He told her he didn't want to be dishonest—there was someone else he'd like to date.

As for those phone calls, Sheldon didn't think they were so innocent. "Jen didn't introduce us so we could be great friends!" he always says.

Sheldon says those phone calls gave him the courage to finally ask me on a real date. He planned to find me in the common area where students gathered between classes. On the appointed day he spotted me in a group of people and patiently waited to catch me alone. To kill some time he picked up one of the old-school pay phones on the wall and started a fake conversation. As he turned around to see if the group had broken up, he was shocked to see me walking away hand in hand with my long-distance boyfriend who'd come for a visit. *What's this all about?!* he thought as I walked by without even seeing him.

Luckily for Sheldon, though, that relationship ended over Christmas break. After coming back to campus, I asked a mutual friend what was going on with that hunky baseball player. "Do NOT tell him I'm asking about him," I said, "but I'm just wondering if he's still dating that cute girl he's been seeing forever."

Of course, my friend walked down the block and began the conversation like this: "Guess who's asking about you?!" My cover was blown before I even knew it.

We did some sleuthing back and forth, and Sheldon discovered I was planning to be at a basketball game on campus one night. When I left the arena after the game, I found a note on my windshield. My car may or may not have been illegally parked rather close to the entrance, but in any case, the baseball player had found it and left a note inviting me to a local restaurant. I had studying to do, so I drove to the restaurant just off campus and returned the note to his car, inviting him to join me in the library. I'm pretty sure it was his first visit!

The note (which still exists) was traded back and forth on our windshields until I showed up at the baseball field one day to see him in action. Having grown up a die-hard football fan, I always found baseball slow and boring. But if that's what this guy was going to be doing all semester, I was going to have to at least feign some interest. I had no idea how to conduct myself. Was I supposed to cheer for my favorite player, or play it cool? Would there be a halftime show like in football? Where were the snacks?

We started chatting on the phone again, and after a few more months of feeling out each other's intentions, it was time for our first official date.

As the night approached, I had all my walls up. This guy was too handsome to be a good guy. Some of the athletes had reputations as players OFF the field, and I lumped him in with them. He proposed dinner at his place and a Christian concert at nearby Virginia Military Institute (VMI). I assumed he'd be picking me up, so I was astonished when he called to discuss what time I'd be arriving.

"Dinner will probably be ready about six so we can get on the road for the concert with plenty of time," he said. "Can you make it by then?"

Um, no . . . that's not how it works.

"What?" I said, with a note of surprise in my voice. "Um, no, I was expecting you to pick me up. What time will you be here?"

Sheldon said he'd be right over. What I didn't know was

that I'd thrown a major wrench in his plans. His wonderful roommate, whom we affectionately call "Buck," took over the dinner preparations and Mr. Baseball sped over to pick me up. When we got back to his place, I was treated to grilled chicken, broccoli casserole, and some rolls. He also bought me a rose. (Whoa!) Still, my defenses were on high alert. As I snooped around the apartment looking for warning signs, I found highly suspicious items like . . . the soundtrack to *The Little Mermaid*. Who were these guys trying to fool? I wasn't buying the goody-goody act.

Soon we were off for a mini road trip to VMI, complete with a mixtape he'd made himself. As we talked, I learned that Sheldon was the youngest of six in a hardworking, humble family who lived in a Pennsylvania town with one stoplight. He seemed earnest, genuine, and nervous. After an hour of driving, we found parking on campus and started navigating our way to the concert venue. By this time we were so engrossed in conversation that he walked right into a tension wire securing a telephone pole into the ground. I felt horrible when I looked up and saw the bloody cut on his forehead, but I was also a little flattered that he'd been so distracted.

Now, if you've never been to a Christian concert, you should know that it's a relatively chummy affair. The singer will often spend as much time talking and sharing between songs as he will actually singing them. There's a real sense of community, and most attendees consider themselves brothers and sisters by default, even if they've never met. During the evening, I started hoping this would be one of those concerts where the singer asks everyone to hold hands and sing together at the end. (Wait a minute! What am I talking about?! No attachments! No emotions!) Sure enough, we ended the concert by joining hands, and I didn't want to let go.

I spent the drive back thinking about all the hidden flaws Sheldon must have and how I'd never see him again after graduation in a few months. The *Little Mermaid* thing was obviously a setup, so I had to keep my head on straight. And yet, I felt so drawn to him. When he stopped the car in front of my house, I waited (and waited and waited) for him to get out, open my door, and walk me to the porch.

"I had a great time," he said, still sitting in the driver's seat.

"Me too!" I said, followed by an awkward silence.

After a few more attempts at wrapping things up, it became clear he wasn't going to escort me to the door, so I finally let myself out and went inside. I guess he wasn't as into me as I'd thought. Sheldon later told me that he'd missed my hint because he was "on cloud nine" and couldn't wait to get home and tell his roommates that he'd found the woman he wanted to marry.

The next day was Valentine's Day and I went to church with a longtime male friend of mine. Sheldon saw us there together and assumed it was some kind of "church date" situation. (Side note, ladies: it never hurts for a single man to think he's got a little competition.) It was totally platonic, but it provoked action. A quick call and conversation clarified the situation, and from then on out Sheldon and I were inseparable. Just when I'd decided I no longer needed a man, the perfect one for me showed up.

When he invited me to meet his family in Pennsylvania over Easter break, it felt like a huge step for a relationship only a few weeks old. But Sheldon assured me that everyone would be excited to meet me and we'd have a great time. All during the drive I pumped him for information. "What's your mom like? What about your dad? Who's your favorite sibling? Who's going to be there?" My questions—and my nerves—were endless.

When we pulled up at the house, I refreshed my lip gloss and prepared for the onslaught of hugs and conversation. Only, that's not what happened.

As we approached the front door, I peeked inside through the glass windowpane and saw that just about everyone was sound asleep in front of the TV—including Mr. Bream, who was passed out in his undershirt. There was no welcoming committee, no fanfare, which felt inconceivable to me, having grown up in a household where everyone who comes to the front door is treated like a visiting head of state. Not so with the Breams. Everyone is even-keeled and unimpressed. They work hard and don't get too excited about anything. It's what drew me to Sheldon—his steadiness and calm.

I spent that weekend feeling like I'd landed on another planet. The Breams don't do anything small. A basic family gathering draws a crowd of twenty-five people, and holidays can hover around eighty. I barely knew Sheldon, and here I was trying desperately to piece together the names and faces of dozens of people. Other than the deeply uniting core of our shared faith, everything else felt foreign—the faces, the food, the traditions—and I'm pretty sure they saw my

Southern self as an oddity too. I wasn't sure I'd ever fit into this world.

I remember calling my mom on the verge of tears and saying, "Everything is just so different!" It wasn't like I'd fallen for someone from another continent—I'd simply crossed the Mason-Dixon Line! But Sheldon took me out of my comfort zone and made me question my independent streak. I was rethinking the kind of life I wanted to have. Maybe I didn't want to be a loner after all.

Despite that bumpy weekend and a later attempt to break things off when I felt they were getting too serious too fast, I couldn't deny that I was falling in love. What to do? I was headed home to attend law school at Florida State University, but all of a sudden this "no strings attached" relationship had developed some strings. Sheldon and I spent every minute together we could leading up to graduation. When the day came, I couldn't even introduce him to my family. The baseball team was in a conference playoff, which meant the senior guys wouldn't be on campus to walk across the stage and collect their diplomas.

By that point, Sheldon had asked what I thought about him moving to Tallahassee. We would spend the summer apart—me in Washington, DC, him in Atlanta—but he was willing to find his way to Tallahassee by the time I started classes in the fall.

I had a high school friend who was working in FSU's

athletic department, so we decided to start Sheldon's search there. They didn't have any full-time staff positions with benefits, but they could use some hourly help. It wasn't much, but it was a start. The paycheck was so slim that my parents offered to let Sheldon stay with them. So there we were, me living with a roommate near the law school campus, and Sheldon living thirty minutes away with my family. I'm sure my parents loved keeping an eye on him on the rare occasion when he wasn't working long hours at the office.

Sheldon loved everything about the world of college sports and threw himself into any assignment he could pick up. At any hour of the day or night, you could find him at a women's golf tournament or handling autograph requests for then–football coach Bobby Bowden. He was making almost no money, had no benefits, and worked nonstop—and he loved it.

It's a good thing he stayed so busy, because year one of law school left me absolutely shell-shocked. I'd always been a solid student with proven study habits, but law school stretches you to another level. The amount of material I had to get through on a given day was overwhelming. It was the first time I doubted my ability to keep up, let alone stay at the top of the class. Everyone in law school had been a top student before they got there.

Without Sheldon and my roommate, Stacy, I would've given up. Every time I felt crushed by the workload, Sheldon would remind me of other obstacles I'd overcome. "Don't give up now," he'd say. "It'll all be worth it in the end."

There was plenty of gallows humor along the way. At one point Stacy's and my answering machine (back when those were a thing) directed people to contact Dr. Kevorkian's office if they couldn't find us. Our budgets were so tight and our days so filled with trying to survive that we actually had our power turned off more than once. And guess what? Our professors didn't care. They'd heard it all before and expected us to be adults who could manage our own lives.

The culture was another radical shift from my years at Liberty. I couldn't understand how some of my fellow students could get drunk on consecutive weeknights and still survive the gauntlet of that first year. (The truth was, many of them didn't.) I came to realize that our professors weren't there to walk us through our personal crises. In fact, they'd rather not hear about them.

I was back to feeling like an absolute outsider. I didn't party. I wasn't one of the cool kids. And I ate all my feelings. Stressed? Relieved? Terrified? Exhausted? Overwhelmed? They all meant the same thing: time for some carbs. So, in addition to earning a reputation as the class goody-goody, I also packed on fifteen pounds, which made me feel even more depressed.

The one class where I felt I was doing well was Legal Research and Writing. I liked the process of putting together a case in the written word. Our primary assignment was to write a full-fledged legal brief, a document that took an entire semester to master. My feedback on the written assignment was consistently good, which felt like a welcome respite. But my happy buzz came to a screeching halt when I realized we'd have to make oral arguments to defend that brief. Not only that, we'd have to be fully prepared to argue the opposing side just as persuasively.

This wasn't like a pageant interview, where I knew all the answers well because they were all my opinions. This would be about knowing every possible case ever decided on these issues and the ability to pivot on a dime before a panel of experienced judges who held my grade in their hands. It was terrifying. I showed up at my professor's office in tears. She wasn't taking the bait. Everyone had to do it, and no amount of crying was going to make a difference. I would have to get it together immediately.

Sheldon, Stacy, my parents—they were all confident that I could do it. "Shan, you're smart and you're great with words," Sheldon prodded. "You've spoken to millions of people on live TV. You're gonna nail this."

So I tackled it the only way I knew how: hours of preparation and plenty of prayer. Once I realized there was no getting away from it, I embraced the process. Many of my classmates seemed completely unfazed. I couldn't tell if it was justified confidence or blissful ignorance. Either way, I didn't plan on being caught off guard. I felt as if I couldn't breathe when I walked into that first round of arguments, but knowing everyone else had to do it made me feel just the tiniest bit better.

Unfortunately, this wasn't a onetime thing. There were cuts along the way. Every time you did well, it meant you'd have to return for the next round. I'm competitive and I wanted to get the best grade possible, so I found this to be the sharpest of two-edged swords. Yes, I needed to advance, but no, I didn't want to develop a bleeding ulcer. And then it was down to four. The final competition would be argued at the Florida Supreme Court, with a couple of the actual justices sitting in. Having argued both sides, I knew the strengths and weaknesses of the case from every angle.

The moment was like so many others in life. You have no choice but to put one foot in front of the other. I prayed fervently that I would have excellent recall and avoid embarrassing myself in front of the students, faculty, and family members who had gathered there. If you've ever seen the stuttering lawyer scene in *My Cousin Vinny*, you can imagine what I was envisioning: an attorney who has such a spectacular meltdown in the courtroom, the entire case falls apart.

But the argument portion passed by in a flash, and it was off to the banquet to celebrate. I couldn't really gauge how I had done, and I didn't care. It was over without a fiasco, and that's all that mattered to me.

When I look back on law school, it feels like three years of exhaustion and sheer terror. I'm not someone who loved it or enjoyed the process. So I'm still baffled that I somehow won the award for Best Oral Advocate that first year. I'd just won my first case at the Florida Supreme Court . . . sort of. Back at Liberty, I had worried about carrying a serious relationship into law school, but there's absolutely no way I would have survived that year without Sheldon.

Little did I know, things were about to get a whole lot tougher for both of us.

Life Is Too Short to Ignore Brownies Forever

Having survived my first year of law school, I began to feel like my old self again. Slowly, I allowed myself to enjoy a few things outside of the grind of studying night and day. When I heard about an opportunity to get my tuition paid while working in the Florida State Legislature, I applied right away. The Capitol was just a couple of blocks from the law school, and totally up my alley. After being accepted into the program, I began juggling classes in the morning with afternoons working in the office of the Florida Speaker of the House.

As if my plate wasn't full enough, I also began to think about coming out of pageant retirement. Competition seemed like a good way to help me lose those extra pounds I'd picked up my first year. During year one of law school, I'd gone into a bit of a shell trying to survive the onslaught of real academic challenges and the lack of connection with many of my classmates. I needed a good personal challenge.

I couldn't return to the Miss America system and hadn't previously considered Miss USA a serious possibility. It's unapologetically a beauty pageant, with no talent competition and no scholarship aspect to it. At five seven I knew I'd be shorter than most of the women competing, but at least I wouldn't have to touch a piano.

There was no way I was going to take a break from school, though, like I'd done when I was Miss Virginia. I reached out to the Miss Florida USA team to determine what level of commitment they would expect. I was told, "The year is what you make it. We keep our titleholder as busy as she'd like to be." That sounded manageable. It felt ridiculous to consider winning a second state title, and I knew the odds were stacked against me. At that point, there wasn't a lot of crossover between the Miss America and Miss USA systems. Many of the competitors and organizers considered the other program to be inferior. Ultimately, I thought the challenge would be good for me.

Between classes, studying, my job, and working out to get in shape for Miss USA, there was little time for sleep. But I felt myself coming out of the fog that had a settled over me that first year, when my confidence had taken a serious blow. Yet I had also started to feel like there was no scenario in which I could see myself practicing law for the rest of my life.

I enjoyed the intellectual jousting, but it seemed there was always a gray area in how the decisions were made. The very same set of facts could lead to very different results based on the way the arguments were framed. I had always thought of the law as a set formula: take a dispute, apply the law, and you'll always get the same result. Yet it often seemed cases were decided based on the judicial philosophy of whichever judge got assigned. That didn't sit well with me. How could respected members of the bench see things so differently? I'm someone who believes in black-and-white answers and a few absolute truths. But I was learning that a career in law wasn't necessarily about that. Why should I spend my life tracking my day in six-minute, billable increments when there was no guarantee that the "good guys" were going to win? I was happy to start there, but determined that I wouldn't stay long.

I will always remember the day when a classroom packed full of my fellow students debated *Roe v. Wade* and the arguments surrounding the legality of abortion. I had looked forward to an honest, spirited conversation, but instead, I heard only one side. Student after student talked about the necessity of making sure that women didn't have to go through with unwanted pregnancies, no matter the circumstance. I kept waiting for someone to responsibly discuss the other side of the debate, if only to make things interesting. I was semistunned when it appeared that no one actually thought there was a single valid argument on the other side.

Thirty minutes into the conversation, I finally decided to stand up. "What about people who believe that life begins at conception? That there's a heartbeat before most women know they're pregnant? That you might be talking about two lives at some point and not just one?"

The whole room looked at me like I had just landed from Mars. If nothing else, I think my classmates had come to respect me as someone who was intelligent and reasoned. The looks on their faces said they couldn't square that with the words that were coming out of my mouth. Their responses told me they hadn't had a healthy debate about compelling state interests and the growing body of science that was telling us more about what happens in the womb. I wasn't there to persuade anyone, but I thought no legal debate had any real value if only one side was represented. Especially on a question that important.

The next day, there was a note in my mailbox from a fellow student. As a devout Catholic, he wrote, he was ashamed that he hadn't stood to join me in that conversation. He apologized for leaving me standing there alone. It was so kind of him, and the whole experience was very eye-opening for me.

When I asked for a week off from work, I didn't tell anyone it was to go compete in the Miss Florida USA pageant. I figured if it didn't go well, I wouldn't have to answer any questions. I didn't feel the same pressure I'd had five years earlier when I competed at the state level for the first time. It might be a tad embarrassing to put myself out there and not even make the finals, but I felt pretty lighthearted about giving it a try.

When I showed up for the competition in July 1994, I discovered several of the women were already working as professional models and actresses, and it showed. The legs and hair were long and sleek. This was a fun bunch, and the competitive jabs were minimal. Everyone seemed to be having a genuinely good time. My fellow contestants joked around as we rehearsed dance numbers and were bused all over town for photo and video shoots and dinners. It seemed many of them had entered on a whim, just to have the experience. It was such a stark contrast to my time in the Miss America system where everyone had prepared for months or years to take on the challenge.

We each had one-on-one interview time with the judges, after first delivering a short speech introducing ourselves in front of the other contestants. I'd prepared my usual semi-serious speech about studying law, and so on, but quickly ditched it when I heard the other presentations. These women were funny and relaxed. No one wanted to hear about my torts class!

Sheldon, my family, and I spotted at least two top contenders who we thought would win it all. I didn't know what to expect. All week long, there were no preliminary awards or scoring feedback from the judges, so you had no idea who the judges liked. I spent my individual time with the judges talking about legislative initiatives and my time working in the Florida House. They seemed engaged, but I wasn't sure playing the brainiac was the best strategy in this glamorous pageant. I didn't come across as sexy or carefree as most of the competitors. I still had (and probably always will have) a bookworm vibe going on, and I didn't know how that was being perceived.

Despite going in blind, I made the first cut, and then the next and the next. The night was a blur until we were down to the final five, being serenaded one at a time. As the crooner belted out All-4-One's "I Swear," each of us had a moment in the spotlight as we tried to appear natural, yet delighted, by this musical interlude. It's slightly awkward to stare into the eyes of the performer as he walks from contestant to contestant singing about loving you forever, buying time for the judges to make their final decisions.

I looked down at the judges' table. They were all shuffling papers and whispering in each other's ears as we tried to read their expressions. The two top contenders were still onstage, so I had no great expectations. One was about five ten, a sunny blonde with not an ounce of fat and plenty of "it" factor. The other, a five-foot-eleven brunette, had already scored roles on major television series. But when those two women were named runners-up, I started to think I had a chance. I was so grateful to make it this far after hanging up my rhinestones five years earlier. This time, when my name was called as the new Miss Florida USA, I knew what I was getting into.

I returned to work and school, never mentioning that I'd picked up a ticket to Miss USA. I remember someone in my office heard about it eventually and offered me a stunned congratulations. Back then you could keep a secret for a few days before the news went viral. I don't think most of my classmates ever found out. Most days, I showed up for class in sweats and makeup free.

My class load as a second-year law student was a little easier, but now I was juggling both my job at the Capitol and appearances as Miss Florida USA. I'm not sure why I thought tackling all that at once was a good idea, but it pushed me to go beyond what I thought were my limits.

No matter where I was, I got in at least an hour workout every day and pretty much stopped eating anything I enjoyed. I knew the Miss USA competition would be fierce, and there's nothing like the thought of wearing a bikini on national television to stop you from eating a pint (or bite) of ice cream. I must confess, with just a teeny bit of guilt, that I actually smiled when a classmate of mine pulled me aside to say he was worried that I'd gotten too thin. He knew nothing about what I was preparing for, but I assured him it was a temporary state. Life is too short to ignore brownies forever.

Sheldon was my rock during that crazy year, and my motivator when I thought I couldn't lift another rep or dig through yet another case. He showed up at every workout with me, cheering me on when I thought I'd reached my limits. "Come on," he'd say, "you can finish this set—just three more!"

When Christmas arrived, we finally took a break to visit his family. All I wanted to do was sleep . . . and visit Hershey Park. Having been raised by a self-described chocoholic, I'd always wanted to visit the one theme park in the country that's dedicated to the stuff. On the drive there, Sheldon kept giving me Hershey kisses from his pocket. The man doesn't eat chocolate, so I'm not sure how we fell in love.

When we finally got to the park, the sun was setting, and, boy, was it cold. If you've never been, the whole place actually *smells* like chocolate. They have to be piping that in, right? As we stood bundled up and shivering in line for the carousel, we spotted a man on the ride get on one knee, open a ring box, and propose. The whole crowd buzzed with excitement! But when the couple rotated back around, she still had her gloves on and they were both seated and looking away from each other. I looked at Shel, "Whoa, that didn't go well."

What I didn't know at the time was that Sheldon had a ring for me in his pocket and was planning to propose on that very same carousel! He later told me that when he saw that couple crash and burn, "Complete panic set in."

We eventually found our way to Santa's Workshop, where the "elves" were busy whipping up hot chocolate for the freezing visitors. It was exactly what I was looking for.

The lights glittering in the trees, the quaint shops, Sheldon handing me the last Hershey kiss in his pocket—and suddenly he was down on one knee. As I removed the wrapper from that misshapen candy he'd just given me, I realized it wasn't chocolate. It was a ring.

"Will you be my wife?" Sheldon said.

WHAT?!!

"Yes!" I said.

There would be no repeat of what happened to the couple on the carousel. By the time we got back to his parents' house, we'd already picked a date and started planning the wedding.

Just a few weeks later, it was time to head off to the Miss USA Pageant. Without giving away too much, I told my professors I'd need to be out and worked with them on making sure I didn't miss too much classwork. The pageant organizers had sent a thick packet of preparation materials, and I hadn't had much time to pore through it before I took off. At my connecting airport I spotted several of my fellow competitors—easily—because they were wearing their crowns and sashes. (Apparently, we were supposed to do that for our arrival.) Eeek. I hoped there weren't too many other important instructions I'd missed.

After arriving in South Padre Island, Texas, we quickly began rehearsals and taped some scenes for the upcoming live broadcast. It was February and freezing, but we posed on the beach as if it was 100 degrees.

At one point in the shoot, someone in the crew asked, "Is there anyone here who rides horses?" I grew up riding, so I raised my hand.

The next thing I knew, I was galloping down the beach bareback in a bikini as the chilly ocean surf splashed me head to toe. I wouldn't recommend doing this with a horse you've known for thirty seconds, without a saddle or any real feel for just how fast you're going to be going. My mom has a picture of this moment, I suspect one of her favorites. I see a smile on my face and terror in the pit of my stomach every time I look at it.

Also terrifying? The twenty-five-foot staircase that we had to walk down for the evening gown portion of the competition. It was metallic and slick, with no handrails. The producers kept it onstage during rehearsals and downtime so we could get the feel for descending, but even in my running shoes, I felt like I had vertigo every time I stood at the top. How in the world would I navigate this thing in slippery stilettos next week? It seemed improbable. They told us that cadets from the nearby United States Air Force Academy would be lining the stairs on the final night—but that they'd be holding up sabers, so we shouldn't expect to be able to lean on them. (Or their sabers.) How comforting!

When it came time to meet the judges for interviews, I realized that this setup was also going to be . . . challenging. Several contestants shared the space, sitting at tables just a couple of feet apart. We sat down for a three-minute, one-on-one conversation with each judge, but you could tell that you were competing for their attention. When a bell rang, you said your good-byes and moved to the next table.

I couldn't have been more thrilled when I sat down across from my old childhood "friend," world-famous radio host Casey Kasem! Dare I tell him about my sneaky Sunday nights, listening to him on my Walkman under the covers? I quickly decided that it wouldn't be in my best interest to spend the measly 180 seconds I had with him coming off like a crazed stalker. Instead, we talked about what it really meant to be successful in life. It was tough to ignore the contestant across the room who decided to break into an opera solo.

All in all, I didn't think I did well in these interviews. The judges were all celebrities and Hollywood types, and my résumé probably came off more like a ninety-year-old librarian than a sexy swimsuit model. I wasn't sure where I'd land, but at every step I asked the Lord to give me peace and take me only as far as He wanted me to go.

If God really was behind this crazy quest, something I'd started to convince myself of, he had provided me with one very important miracle: my roommate. Without knowing a thing about our connection, the pageant organizers had put me with a woman named Susan, Miss Virginia, whom I already knew from Liberty. We both marveled at our good fortune. We could navigate the stress together!

When wearing a swimsuit in public on a regular basis, one becomes an expert in self-tanners. Both my parents are melanoma survivors and I spent too many years soaking up the Florida sun. As a result, I have regular checkups, have had many spots removed, and am familiar with every faux tanner under the sun. If you want to know which ones will turn you orange and which ones look like you just spent a week in Tahiti, I'm your girl.

Every other night, Susan and I would strip down—one in the bathroom, one in the bedroom—and slather ourselves with our tanning potions. We'd laugh and talk through the tedious process of waiting for the goop to dry. We made other lifelong friends along the way, too: Chandelle from Nebraska and Paulette from Georgia.

I'd left my engagement ring with Sheldon so it wouldn't seem like I wasn't serious about becoming Miss USA. But once I decided I could trust this trio, I revealed my secret. "I'm already engaged," I whispered. They were each excited and understood my decision to keep it quiet.

Having made peace with the staircase from Hades, I was ready for the final night. There were rumors swirling around that certain states would definitely make the finals because their TV markets were so important for ratings. I hoped that wasn't true but figured it could work in my favor because Florida does have millions of people scattered from Pensacola to Key West. I was one of the last names called, but I made the first cut.

Swimsuit was up next. Here's the thing most people don't know: the wardrobe people choose the suits, not the contestants. When the wardrobe mistress handed me two tiny pieces of red fabric, I politely said, "Oh, this isn't my size. I'm going to need some more material." She replied, "Nope, Florida, that's what we've assigned you. Work with it." Yikes. I could only pray my pastor wouldn't be watching. They gave us color-coordinated scarves to swish around, and of course mine caught on my heel as I was trying to strut my stuff across the stage. Not my finest moment, but I'd been through worse.

After evening gown and a quick chat with the host, our group was cut to six. I survived, which meant it was now time to face the judges' questions. I drew a name out of a bowl, and it fell to the hunky soap star to quiz me. He asked me about the concept of taking children away from mothers who were dependent on welfare. *Wait a second*, I thought, *I'm pretty sure you didn't draft that yourself.* What about my favorite color or something? I talked about the need to reform the documented corruption within the welfare system and tried to shut down any proposal that would take children away from their parents. The other finalists answered questions about celebrities' personal views and whether prayer belongs in schools.

There was a commercial break, and we all stood onstage waiting to find out who would make the final three. I felt such a strange peace at that point, not a single bit of nerves. I prayed, *Lord, whatever you want to happen here, it's in your hands.*

Later, and he fully admits this, I found out Sheldon was actively rooting against me. If I won, it would mean moving to Los Angeles for a year of nonstop travel, hardly ever coming home to see him. Now that he saw this thing was within reach, he started to grow concerned. To this day, he jokes that he thought I'd "run off with a movie star" and forget all about him.

Sheldon got his wish. I wasn't among the final three. I had no regrets and knew it was all for a reason. The final three all had to answer the same question, "What advice would you give First Lady Hillary Clinton?" In the years since that night, I've thought a million times about how my answer to that question could've hurt my ability to be respected as an objective journalist covering politics and campaigns. Clinton had taken a lot of criticism in those days for playing such an active role in pushing health care reform. Anything I might have said that night as a twenty-four-year-old law student would almost certainly have been replayed over and over once I stepped into the world of straight news reporting. But I'd soon find out that wasn't the only reason I wasn't destined to become Miss USA.

The Darkest Cloud

When I returned to school, it was like the Miss USA Pageant never happened. Only a couple of my classmates even knew I'd been away at the competition, and there was plenty of catching up to do academically when I wasn't making public appearances as Miss Florida. Work at the Capitol became my favorite part of the day, and after months of toiling away in a basic cubicle, my coworkers had managed to get me my own, grown-up office. At night, Sheldon and I would work on the wedding plans for December and talk about the life we wanted to build.

Around this time, Sheldon had been battling an ear problem that just wouldn't seem to clear up. He felt like he was losing some of his hearing, and there was an irritating ringing that kept getting worse. He didn't have insurance, but one of the team doctors at Florida State was kind enough to examine him and prescribe some rounds of antibiotics. Still, the mystery dragged on for months.

He finally sought out an ear, nose, and throat doctor who examined him and said there was a long-shot diagnosis they needed to rule out: a brain tumor. The doctors assured us that there was very little chance a twenty-four-year-old in peak physical condition would suddenly develop something so grave, so we scheduled the testing and put it to the back of our minds.

The next week, I was happily moving into my first official office when Sheldon called. Looking back, I've always been grateful that God provided me a private space for taking what would become the most devastating call of my life.

"Shan, I need to come see you in person," Sheldon said with a steady voice.

My heart began to race. I knew what that meant. "No, tell me right now," I said. "Whatever you need to say." I knew the waiting would be torture for both of us, and I already expected the worst.

Sheldon calmly laid out what the doctor had found. "I've got a brain tumor the size of a golf ball wrapped around my hearing nerve." I felt like I couldn't breathe. For months we thought he was dealing with an ear infection. The reality was something beyond our worst-case scenario.

"You're going to be okay," I willed myself to say, but I felt devastated. When we hung up, I closed the door of my office and sobbed.

The news came at a time I was still digesting the idea of actually getting married. As much as I loved Sheldon, and as happy as we were to be engaged, I'd always felt anxious about marriage itself. My parents were divorced, and I hated being caught in the middle of that. I worried, too, that my independent streak would complicate the role I thought all wives had to play. To me, marriage meant someone telling you what to do or how you could spend your paycheck. But all that changed with Sheldon's diagnosis. Suddenly, I was faced with the possibility of losing him. That reality check hit me hard.

We were young and in love, but real life was intruding in a way we never could have imagined. This felt like a life-or-death fight, never mind the financial avalanche of treatments whose costs could run well into the hundreds of thousands of dollars. I wanted to quit school, give up my job and Miss Florida USA title, and run to the courthouse to get married. Of course, we both knew that was impossible. I needed to keep moving toward the things that would eventually give us a financial foundation and some stability. Suddenly, I was thrilled that I hadn't been chosen as Miss USA. God had put me just where I'd needed to be.

Sheldon had no health insurance, and we were living hundreds of miles away from his tight-knit family. He immediately started looking for a job with better benefits, knowing he'd need to inform them up front that he was facing a major medical event. It broke my heart to see him realize he'd have to leave a job he loved so much. He still looks back wistfully on those years of low pay, no benefits, and endless hours because he was right in the middle of what he loved most: top-level collegiate athletic competition. He put in far more than his required hours and always marveled he was so lucky to be in that position. But short of a miracle, the financial burden of what he was facing would wipe him out for years to come.

Tallahassee is blessed with an abundance of state jobs, which are steady and come with great benefits, and Sheldon had skills any good employer would be after: attention to detail, solid work ethic, organization, and most important, unwavering integrity. As Sheldon went through the interview process at the secretary of state's office, he was blunt about his diagnosis. We'd been told that his tumor was slow growing and we had some time to get him situated in a new job before locking in a doctor and getting the surgery scheduled. So he told them he would work as long and hard as he could before the surgery and return as soon as he was well enough to do so. He got the job.

After researching local hospitals in Tallahassee, we set up an initial appointment with a surgeon. He was young and seemed to be a smoker—an odd lifestyle for a doctor—but he knew all about the specific tumor Sheldon had: an acoustic neuroma. When we asked how many times he'd performed the surgery, though, his answer was in the single digits. It didn't seem like a lengthy track record, but we didn't know exactly what else to ask. I left the appointment in tears, but not Sheldon. The doctor had said he was almost certain the tumor was benign. That was all Sheldon needed to hear.

Sheldon's cousin Doug happened to be a physician in Pennsylvania. He cautioned us to look for a surgeon who was much more experienced. We found one in Pennsylvania, but Sheldon's insurance company refused to let us pursue an out-of-state option. We eventually learned about a world-class neurosurgeon in Gainesville. He was a professor at the University of Florida and was considered a pioneer in the surgery Sheldon needed.

Dr. Albert Rhoton's secretary was very kind when Sheldon called, but he was taken aback when she laughed at his question, "Do you have any neurosurgeons who perform acoustic neuroma surgeries?"

She went on to explain that Dr. Rhoton had taught the surgery all over the world and performed it hundreds of times. She asked us to send all the tests and films we had so far but cautioned us that Dr. Rhoton couldn't take every case that came across his desk. We understood and started praying: "Please, Lord, let this man take Sheldon's case. We know he's the best of the best and we ask you to open this door."

By this time, Sheldon's story had spread well beyond our immediate family and friends. I remember opening a card at work one day from a church in Alabama. They'd heard about Sheldon through a friend of a friend and wanted to let us know they'd added him to their prayer list. They were complete strangers, sharing our burden. All we wanted was for Sheldon to get the kind of medical care that would give him a fighting chance.

After weeks of waiting for the phone to ring, we got a matter-of-fact call announcing that Dr. Rhoton had taken our case. How soon could we get to Gainesville to meet with him? We thanked God for the good fortune of leading us to this man—truly one of the best in the world at doing what we needed, and incredibly kind. As we moved ahead with surgery plans, I studied for my second-year exams and looked ahead to a summer clerkship in Columbia, South Carolina.

Then, around Mother's Day we got a call from Pennsylvania that Sheldon's father wasn't feeling well. Like all the Breams, he's a tough cookie who doesn't like receiving help, so we were alarmed when we found out he was headed to the hospital. He'd long been treated for chronic lymphatic leukemia, and his regular blood work and doctor's visits should've caught anything seriously wrong with him. But somehow all that constant monitoring had missed something even more threatening that was going on in his body.

The thought of adding any new crisis to Sheldon's plate was overwhelming, especially because he'd had a complicated relationship with his father growing up. As the youngest of six children, Sheldon had been a handful—the family comedian and somewhat oblivious to rules. Sheldon's father was reserved and quiet, making them complete opposites. It led to regular clashes, but once Sheldon left for college, their relationship steadily improved. As he matured, Sheldon understood why his father was the way he was. It sparked him to work on being the man his father wanted him to be. They began to meet each other halfway and became much closer over the years.

Weeks after the new diagnosis, Sheldon's father passed away with Sheldon by his bedside. Life felt crushing, suffocating. All summer, I tried to hide my tears at the law firm where I worked, but I wasn't very successful. As a law student, you want to dazzle the attorneys where you're clerking, not come off as a total basket case. I really had no other option. I managed to choke out that I needed to leave for my fiancé's father's funeral—and oh yeah, I didn't tell you he's got a brain tumor himself. Two of the senior female attorneys took me to lunch, seeming genuinely concerned about the tornado I was living through.

Within weeks, a date had been scheduled for Sheldon's surgery: July third. Although Dr. Rhoton believed the mass was benign, he wouldn't be able to tell us for sure until he actually sent a sample for analysis. He also warned us that the surgery could leave Sheldon deaf in one ear or cause paralysis in the facial nerves that allow him to smile, blink, and make other expressions. We both thought the same thing: Who cares about a little paralysis if he lives through it? We never seriously considered that possible outcome.

Sheldon's mom, Jouetta, and his sister, Theresa, traveled south for the surgery. My parents had driven down, too. We all stayed at a hotel across the street from the hospital that was full of other families there for the same reason. We were advised the delicate procedure could take roughly six hours, and they'd update us when they could.

Before Sheldon went in, hospital staff came to us to discuss things like a living will, power of attorney, and so on. Though we were building our future together, I had no legal status in Sheldon's life. That meant Jouetta, who had just weeks before buried her husband of nearly forty-three years, was now signing papers outlining possible scenarios in which she could lose her youngest child. A woman of deep faith, she was solid and steady throughout the entire ordeal. She prayed often and always said, "The good Lord knows what's going on and He's got it under control."

Once the surgery started, Sheldon's and my families shared the waiting room, pacing and praying. There were occasional updates, but everything seemed to be taking much longer than planned. A couple of hours in, a nurse came to tell us they'd finally removed the portion of his skull that would give them access to the tumor. Just that first phase of the surgery took more than twice the expected time because of the density of the bone. It signaled that this was going to be a long day. Finally, after nine hours of waiting, we were told we could see the surgeon.

"We're all done," Dr. Rhoton said with a steadiness in his voice. "And the sample has already been sent to the pathology lab."

"I bet it made a mess when all that sawdust fell out of his skull," my dad joked, trying to lighten the mood. But the doctor wasn't laughing. He looked exhausted.

The surgery went well, he said, and the tumor appeared benign. But while the doctor's words were technically positive, I knew I wouldn't feel at peace until the lab work finally came back.

Sheldon was in ICU. It was a while before we could see him, even briefly. I tried to prepare myself for seeing my strapping, six-foot-three fiancé lying in a hospital bed. When we finally went into the room, he looked lifeless, hooked to an endless tangle of wires and machines.

All I wanted was to stay there holding his hand and praying for him until he woke up, but we weren't allowed. "You can only see him for a minute or two," the medical staff warned. "Speaking or communicating is going to be stressful and nearly impossible for him at this point, so keep it quick." We kept the visit brief and then slipped out quietly.

Sitting in the hotel room across the street felt like being in jail. We talked, played games, and plotted out a visit to the mall, but I just wanted to be with Sheldon. My heart ached with worry about how he was doing, whether he'd feel abandoned if he woke up alone. Over the next couple of days, the routine continued—quick visits to see him, then being kicked out for several hours. I was concerned about how quickly he seemed to be wasting away and how much pain he was in. He could barely form a sentence and just needed to rest. "Let's go, honey," his mother whispered, "there's no sense in us being here." She was happy to give him some space. I wasn't.

Early on the third morning, he'd been transferred to a private room, and I decided to sneak over and see him by myself. I quietly snuck out of the hotel and jogged across the street. Selfishly, I was tired of people telling me I couldn't stand vigil at his bedside. As I snuck in shortly before dawn his room was dark; only the lights on the machines monitoring his progress were blinking. I didn't want to wake him, so I took a seat and waited for him to wake up. It didn't take long.

He was so quiet at first, I couldn't understand what he was mumbling. Sheldon was clearly in enormous pain and trying to say something. I finally heard him say, "My face." It didn't take long for me to piece together what he was trying to tell me. The complication we hadn't really considered had crashed in overnight. The right side of his face was paralyzed, leaving him with a drooping mouth and the inability to close his right eye. As the sun started to rise and brighten his room, I saw for myself that my handsome fiancé was going to have another hurdle to overcome. He looked as if he'd had a stroke, with one side of his face completely slack and unresponsive.

Doctors had advised us that when the brain swells in reaction to the surgery, it often compresses and damages nerves—sometimes permanently. Each case is different, so we had no idea what to expect. The surgeon counseled us that if the nerves were going to regenerate, we'd see signs within six months. Otherwise, we shouldn't get our hopes up.

"You know I love you no matter what, right?" I assured him. Sheldon had made it through the surgery and we now knew for sure that he'd survive. We would deal with the paralysis and move forward. In such a short time, he'd gone from a twenty-four-year-old on top of the world to a young man with a drastically altered life. There was a dark cloud of depression coming, and neither one of us knew how to deal with it.

By the time Sheldon was able to leave the hospital, he looked like a shell of his former self. His head had been shaved, with enormous metal staples holding together a jagged, bloody scar down the back of his skull. He had lost so much weight, he looked like a skeleton. His balance was off, his speech was slurred, and at times he had to wear a clear plastic wrap over the paralyzed side of his face so that his eye wouldn't be damaged by his inability to blink. Sometimes he said it hurt too bad to even form a thought or a sentence.

It wasn't until much later in this journey that we talked with numerous people who had been through lengthy surgeries under hours of anesthesia, who told us about the enormous dark hole they spiraled down into. I don't know if it's the process of going under the knife or the reality of the aftermath that creates such a perfect storm of despair, but that's exactly what happened to Sheldon.

I remember taking him to the grocery store for some fresh air—his first outing after coming home. Feeling fiercely protective of him, I was furious at the gaping mouths of some of the people we passed in the aisles. As he shuffled along, I wanted to scream at them, "Haven't you ever seen a sick person before! He's not a monster!" Instead, I choked back my tears and prayed he hadn't caught the looks on their faces.

I did everything I could think of, trying to make him feel better physically and emotionally. But as he slowly came to terms with how difficult his recovery was going to be, he pulled further and further away. "I'm never going to look the same," he'd mumble when I tried to reassure him. I could see he was hurting, but nothing that brought him joy before the surgery even seemed to register with him after a while: sports, favorite foods, me. I tried not to feel sorry for myself, but it seemed like even though he'd survived the surgery, I was going to lose him anyway.

At one point I summoned the courage to ask a question that'd been worrying me. "So, do you still want to go ahead as planned for December?"

"I don't care," he said. "Whatever you want . . ."

I longed for miracles of healing, remembering all the people who were praying for us and trying to encourage Sheldon in a job that he merely tolerated. There was nothing inspiring about it, other than the fact that it had saved him from years of crushing debt. That was something to be deeply grateful for, so he went through the motions, performing as a top employee. But I could see that it killed him to go from being on the sidelines of a headline-making game to pushing paper and punching a clock. I took every opportunity that I could to meet him for lunch and give him a break from the monotony.

Months into the ordeal, on a brisk November day, I picked

Sheldon up for a two-for-one lunch at the Pizza Hut buffet. It was a perfect fit for our budget. I had continued planning the wedding for late December, assuming Sheldon's fog would lift enough for him to show up for the ceremony. But with no financial buffer and wedding invoices piling up, every penny mattered.

As I sat across the table from Sheldon that day, I thought I saw the corner of his mouth twitch. My heart raced, but not wanting to get ahead of myself, I acted as if nothing happened and watched for another sign of movement.

Within seconds I saw it again. I took his hand and said, "I think I saw your face move a bit on the right side. Did you feel it?"

"No, I'm not feeling a thing," he said. But the corner of his mouth moved yet again.

I tore through my purse, found my compact mirror, and jammed it into Sheldon's hand. "Yes! I see it too!" he exclaimed, his eyes lighting up. I hadn't been imagining things.

It was the first glimmer of hope we'd had in months. We began jumping up and down in that Pizza Hut and people stared at us with their mouths wide open. I'm sure they thought we were nuts, but we couldn't have cared one single bit.

There was still a long road ahead, but we felt blessed to finally see light at the end of the tunnel. And as I walked down the aisle on December thirtieth, I felt more sure of that decision than any other in my life. I was no longer afraid of marriage, no longer worried that Sheldon wouldn't find his way back to us. At one point in the ceremony I turned around to see his five siblings weeping. They had been through so much: the sudden loss of their father and months of watching Sheldon struggle.

Our college pastor, the late Dr. Jerry Falwell, had agreed to help officiate our ceremony. He'd known us long before this awful year and he took time to acknowledge what Sheldon and his family had faced.

"No one could have foreseen all the trials these last few months would bring into your lives," he said in his booming voice. "You've faced the death of your beloved father and your own mortality, too." As sniffles punctuated the sanctuary, he shifted the tone. "But you've chosen to end this year with a joyous occasion, so let's celebrate!"

It was the easiest yes I'd said in my life.

Losing My Toenails (and My Temper)

My husband does not believe in New Year's resolutions. He *does*, however, set goals that he'd like to achieve, and these have a way of getting made in late December. Several years back he came up with an especially ambitious nonresolution: running a marathon. *Wow*, I thought, *I hope he has a great time with that.*

A former college athlete, Sheldon has always stayed fit, so I knew he'd get it done. If he was feeling antsy, I'd much rather have him taking on the challenge of a superhuman physical endeavor than buying a convertible sports car or suddenly deciding he needed highlights. I envisioned myself making up T-shirts and posters, ferrying a car full of supporters to various points along the route so we could yell our rowdy encouragement.

As I was mentally mapping out our logo and color scheme, Sheldon startled me back to reality. "I want us to do it together." Given that I couldn't run around the block, let alone a distance better suited for a car, I didn't entertain this notion for more than a nanosecond. I told him no.

"I'm serious," he continued. "It's going to take hours of training every week, and I want you to do it with me."

HOURS' worth of running EVERY week? This is what you should know about Sheldon: he's honest to a fault. He made no attempt to massage what he was asking me to do. No couching it in flowery lies about how easy the run would be.

My protests were rapid-fire. "I'll just slow you down." "I don't have the time." Not to mention, "I. Don't. Run." Never mind those details, Sheldon was adamant about this nonresolution, and I had officially been sucked into the plan.

Sheldon bought a book, something along the lines of *Idiot's Guide to Running a Marathon*. I thought that a bit redundant. Wasn't everyone who willingly chose to run 26.2 miles a bit of an idiot? One of the book's first recommendations was to pick a race, sign up, and send in your money. That way, you have an end date to train for. I felt bad about wasting my entry fee because I knew there was no way I was actually going to run the Pittsburgh Marathon. I had already begun laying the groundwork for gracefully bowing out after the first training run or two.

Step two was telling everyone you knew that you were running a marathon. For Sheldon that soon included complete strangers in the grocery checkout line. He's not one to chat up people he doesn't know, but something about this nonresolution was overruling his good sense. I just sort of smiled, nodded, and continued plotting my escape.

The first training run was billed as a "carefree" three-mile jog. For me, I might as well have been scaling Mount Everest. I wheezed and panted, legs on fire and attitude in the crapper. Even this *pretending* for the first week or so was beyond my acting capabilities.

That week, our best friend, Scott, shared his runner's prayer with me: "Lord, you pick 'em up, I'll put 'em down." Catchy, yes, and at times the only lifeline that kept me putting one foot in front of the other. One week stretched into the next and my protests weren't getting me anywhere. For some reason I kept showing up, feeling my competitive nature kicking in.

I would never counsel a beginning runner to do what we did, which was to go from zero to marathon in five months. We had picked the Pittsburgh Marathon because we have lots of family there and thought the weather would be perfect in May. But it left us no slack in the training schedule.

On every punishing run, I found myself vacillating between tamping down the bad words that popped up in my brain and threatened to flood out my lips and praying for the strength to take one more step. I began to lose my toenails, and very often my temper. How did I let myself get dragged into this? It was easily the most physically demanding task I'd ever undertaken, and I was learning it was equally taxing mentally. My shins ached, and it felt like I was spending every free minute I had away from work torturing myself. Yet at every turn, Sheldon cheered us on. "We got this!" he said. "How cool will it be to say we actually ran a marathon?"

A third of the way through training, I got incredibly sick. I feared what would happen if I missed a run, but I physically could not do it, so I spent the time sleeping instead. My next run, two days later, was a revelation. For the first time, I actually felt like a runner. I wasn't fighting through every step. My lungs weren't on the verge of collapse. As an inexperienced runner, I hadn't realized that I needed to listen to my body. It was begging for an opportunity to regenerate, but I didn't know enough to comply.

Then, with a new spring in my step and the halfway mark approaching, I made another rookie mistake. I decided to reward myself with a spa pedicure for my calloused, battered feet. It was pure bliss, and I glided home with my skin as fresh as a newborn's . . . until I went out for my next run.

I quickly realized that those calluses I'd just sloughed off had served a purpose. They had built up a way for my body to cope with the battering it was taking. That's the thing about pain, there's usually some kind of meaning in it. As humans our instinct will always be to run from it, but sometimes you can't escape. That's when you have to embrace the discomfort and find the lesson tucked inside the chaos. When we unearth those valuable nuggets hidden deep inside our hurt, we not only *survive* the valley—we come out of it with new tools (and sometimes calluses). The marathon taught me that I could fight through pain, and that I was tougher than anyone thought—most especially me.

Toward the end of the training, we were getting up at 4:00 a.m. on Saturdays so we could complete runs ranging up to twenty miles. The Florida sun beats down without mercy, and we would make that final turn into our neighborhood soaking wet with sweat. On one occasion some friends of ours were driving by and slammed on the brakes when they saw us. The wife leaned out the window. "What happened?! Are you guys okay?" I was barely able to talk her down from dialing 911.

After a sufficient cooldown, I would spend an hour soaking in the tub. It also became my habit to eat a full sleeve of Oreos during this soak. Math has never been my strong suit, so while I assumed I was burning thousands of calories on these runs and could eat with abandon—such was not the case. I have to be the only person ever to GAIN weight while training for a marathon. True story.

After months of running in pancake-flat Tampa, Florida, we finally made it to marathon day. Not long before we arrived in Pittsburgh, I discovered it was one of the hilliest marathon courses in the country. Put another check in the rookie mistake column. On the drive there, I was a bundle of nerves and anxiety. As part of our deal, Sheldon had promised to stay with me for the full race instead of pushing ahead. My pace was so leisurely that we spent most of the course running side by side with a guy who was jumping rope the entire way for charity.

The first three miles of any run are often the most challenging for me. I'm not sure if my body is trying to get into a rhythm, but that was true on marathon day, too. Before I knew it, though, we were at mile six, then ten, then fourteen. The people of Pittsburgh do an incredible job on marathon day. All along the route there were bands, people cheering and handing out freshly sliced fruit, and shouts of, "You're almost there!" Even when you still have ten miles to go, the crowd keeps you motivated.

I hit a wall around mile nineteen, but there was zero chance I was stopping. Something about all those months of blood, sweat, and tears had lit a fire in me. Short of a broken leg, I was determined to cross the finish line. "By the end of this day, we'll be marathon runners!" Sheldon kept saying.

We kept on plugging, powering through the pain and overriding the impulse to stop moving. Together, we did something I thought was impossible just five months prior.

I never look at the photo of us crossing the finish line. I was flat-out chunky at that point, so I prefer to revisit that moment through my rose-colored memory. The one in which I'm basically a gazelle in size S running shorts.

Sheldon wanted to check running a marathon off his bucket list. Done. One of these days, I'll get him to revisit the Chanel bag that's always been on mine . . .

"You'll Never Make It in This Business"

I threatened to do a cartwheel across the stage when I collected my law degree, but my parents convinced me that it wouldn't look very dignified in a dress and robe. Escaping the three years of torture just seemed worth celebrating in a big way. Sheldon and I were planning a move to Tampa, where I had accepted a position with a firm specializing in employment law. It felt like a perfect fit with my undergraduate degree in management. Sheldon was still in recovery, but we felt like spreading our wings away from family would be a smart thing to do as newlyweds.

Our budget was tight, but we found a beautiful apartment that felt more like a resort, with a state-of-the-art gym and giant, sparkling pool lined with palm trees. That's the thing about living in Florida: sunshine makes everything better. We were happy as clams, just being together and dreaming about the future. Our weekly grocery budget was about $30. A box of pasta, some sandwich fixin's, and cereal—presto. I didn't think anything of it at the time, but when my mom found out years later, she started crying. "Why didn't you come to us for help?" she said. Because we didn't think we needed it!

Thank goodness I married a man who is fiscally responsible. The subject of money has always been an uncomfortable one for me. My family never had a cushion growing up, and finances were a major cause of tension between my parents. I'm grateful for every penny we make—I just get a stomachache when I think about managing it well.

One thing Sheldon and I have never wavered on is tithing. Both of us grew up watching our families commit to giving back out of their modest income; we believe our church manages its resources wisely, pouring into lives and communities in responsible ways. Thinking about finances has always made my blood pressure rise, but even when we barely had enough to cover monthly expenses, our tithe was the one check it didn't scare me to write. In our minds, it's not really our money anyway. If the good Lord has blessed us, even temporarily, in a way that we can help others, why hesitate? I'm not saying it's always been easy, but I am saying God has been faithful.

As I studied my guts out for the bar exam that year, I prayed I wouldn't become the first associate in firm history to fail it. We learned our results would be posted online several weeks later, so as soon as the two-day test concluded, the countdown began. Every day or so I'd hear a rumor the list was up and I'd rush to refresh the screen, only to see it wasn't yet time. I focused on diving into the actual practice of law and quickly learned there's plenty you don't learn in law school. My legal secretary, Sandy, became a teacher and a lifesaver. We're still good friends. There's no telling how many times she saved me from being sanctioned or disbarred while I was figuring out how to do my job, especially when it came to filing all the paperwork that the state requires for every case.

Our office definitely had the vibe of a family, with plenty of support and humor. There was only one partner who really terrified me. He liked to yell and pile on overnight work assignments just when you were finally walking out the door. In time, I learned he was a teddy bear on the inside, but for the first few months, dealing with him felt like facing a firing squad. “Bream! Get in here!” The memory of those words still sends shivers down my spine. But when the news came that I’d passed the bar, that same partner turned to me and quietly said, “I never doubted you would.”

The practice of law was a grind. Any new associate will tell you that. The billable hours that require you to account for your day in six-minute increments, the partners who wait until the last minute to assign you a filing due the next morning, the pressure to bring in new clients—it was an endless churn. Some of my classmates immediately took to it, enjoying the challenges as they came. But I felt like I could never catch my breath. On rare occasions when I managed to take a weekend, Sunday night brought on a level of dread that grew into a suffocating black cloud by Monday morning.

I had gone into this knowing that I wouldn’t practice law for long, and actually doing it confirmed that vision in a million ways. There’s a reason everyone says that if you love what you do, it won’t seem like work. My life felt like a constant fight to jam a square peg into a round hole. It was a good living, honest work, and a solid career. But this could not be my life’s calling.

The one thing I’d always been was a news junkie. I was

hungry for every detail of current events as they were unfolding. Digging into a story, the characters and the motivations, was fascinating to me. I've always been a bit Nancy Drew, never taking anything at face value, always convinced that there's much more to the story. But when I was in college, my dad had made clear to me that he didn't consider journalism a real job. My choices were simple: law school or med school. I know he was trying to make sure I had a future full of options, but as much as I dreaded telling him I wanted to leave my legal career for journalism, I started to wonder if I could really keep on doing this for the rest of my life.

I started sniffing around for information about what a life in journalism would actually be like. By coincidence, our pastor at the time had recommended us to a local news anchor who was doing a story on marriage at all stages. We were the newlyweds. The tapings took place at a local station, and I immediately became enamored with everything I saw and heard. People bustled through the newsroom. Police scanners were buzzing with the latest crime reports around town. The set, with all its bright lights and colors, was mesmerizing.

I asked an endless list of questions and started dreaming about how I could get from where I was to where I wanted to be. I quizzed everyone in the business who would let me buy them lunch or a cup of coffee. "Am I crazy to even consider this?" Sheldon and I spent time talking to people we trusted and praying together among ourselves. "Lord, please guide us—open and close the doors."

My biggest question was whether I should go back to school and get a mass communications degree. Across the board, everyone's answer was the same: no. Diving right into the business would be the best education I could get. But how? I reached out to the local affiliate where Sheldon and I had been interviewed and was told I couldn't volunteer or intern there unless it was officially for college credit. That was my first hurdle, and I was determined to get past it.

I called every community college and university across the state. Nearly every one of them told me I'd have to return to college, take a new round of general education classes, and apply to the communications school before I could become eligible for internship credits. I didn't have that kind of time or patience, so I bombarded professors and deans with my transcripts and pleas for the opportunity to do something a little more nontraditional. I lost count of how many people said no. (Guess what? It's going to happen a lot in life, and you might as well get used to it.) Finally, I landed a meeting at the University of South Florida. We struck a deal: I would take a newswriting class, and the school would allow me to get internship credits at the same time.

And so, the next four months became even busier. I'd work at my firm all day, then spend nights and often weekends at the local ABC affiliate there in Tampa. One reporter in particular, Elaine Quijano, was incredibly gracious to me. She gave me guidance and encouragement—including a physical checklist of things you should do while pursuing a story. She also let me shadow her on the job, so I could see how a real journalist tracked down leads and interviews. Another person, a photographer, allowed me to tag along with him but refused my offer to buy him dinner. Instead, he made me promise that as I progressed through the business,

I would help others along the way. I've never forgotten his kindness or his advice.

I began taking snippets of work to my two primary bosses, asking them for feedback and guidance. Newswriting was a different language from writing for a legal document. Time to ditch the "heretofores" and "prayers for relief" and stick to the who-what-where-when. But I was motivated, and the constructive criticism sharpened my ability to write a script. A couple of months in, my decision was made. There was no clear-cut path, but I knew I had to leave law and fight my way into journalism. When I first announced my plans to the station's news director, he promptly reminded me, "Uh, no one's offered you a job." A minor detail!

I then began to tell the partners at my firm that I was planning to jump ship. One by one they marveled that I was having a midlife crisis at the age of twenty-nine. But a couple said to me, "I always wished I'd pursued a different dream, so I'll be cheering for you." That gave me enough courage to keep moving. Within weeks, I was offered an actual, full-time job at the station. It was a massive pay cut, and the hours were 2:00 a.m. to 11:00 a.m. I couldn't have been happier.

Many of our friends and family truly thought I'd lost it. Why would I abandon my legal training and take on a job that turned my life upside down? My dad was the hardest one to tell. He'd been so proud that I was making my way as a young lawyer, drawing a steady income and following a clear career path. But as I jumped headfirst into this new world, I knew it had been the right choice. Sure, I always felt tired and my social life took a serious hit, but I was starting to feel like I was doing what I'd been meant to do all along. I would answer phones, make coffee, and write some of the scripts for the morning anchors. Soon, I was working the teleprompter. Trust me, this is a critical part of any newscast. Following an anchor's pace and cadence as you roll the words of the scripts across the screen is an art. I had no training before I picked up this task, so I spent many commercial breaks getting dressed down by one of the anchors. "I see what you're doing," she said. "Trying to throw me off!"

Within weeks a producer left and I began taking on some of her duties. All the while, I was still going out with reporters who allowed me to tag along and help in some small way—taking notes and recording my own snippets of material when I could. I continued to badger my bosses for feedback and more responsibilities. One early morning, several months after I started working at the station, I stopped by my mailbox and found a memo from my boss. "We're going to give you a shot as a reporter," he wrote. I would still be responsible for completing my other tasks, but if something broke and the station was short-staffed, there was a chance I'd be called into action. Score!

I still remember my first live shot so clearly. The producer assigned me a story about a controversy over standardized testing in Florida, so I filled my brain with every fact and figure, prepared to give our audience an informed report. It was about 5:30 a.m. and Sheldon promised he would wake up early to watch.

I called him right after my report. "What did you think?"

I know him well enough to know when he's trying to find

a nice way to deliver some unpleasant information. Turns out I'd nailed the content, but my face and voice were as lifeless as a robot's. I was definitely a work in progress.

As more opportunities arose, I would spend an hour after my Friday shift reviewing any reports I'd done during the week. I saw loads of room for improvement, and I was happy to take direction from my more experienced coworkers. Some of them made it clear that I didn't belong there. Tampa is a large television market, and most of the reporters and anchors had worked in smaller markets for years before reaching this point. When I asked for help or guidance, many of them said that if I was going to work in a big market, I should already know the answers to the questions I was asking. Part of me knew they were right, but I was exceedingly grateful for those who decided to help me anyway.

It seemed everyone had an agent, so I asked my coworkers if they had representation. One of the morning anchors connected me with his friend and agent who was going to be in town for the Super Bowl. "I've seen your work, and you've got potential," she said when we first met. I liked her right away and she took a big chance on me. I didn't know it at the time, but weeks later, I'd need her more than ever.

All of a sudden, my boss (and his boss) abruptly left the station. As is often the case in the news business there was really no explanation, just an announcement that management was gone. The new boss showed up and, within days, started putting his stamp on things. Everyone seemed terrified. I wasn't. By that time, I was doing the work of three very different jobs for the same basement salary I'd signed on for months before. I had hours no one else wanted, and the best attitude in the place. When the new boss called me into his office, I expected him to say thank you. Instead, he dropped the hammer.

When you see that the head of Human Resources is sitting in the meeting you've been called into, it's not a good sign. Mr. New Boss proceeded to unload, giving me a speech that went something like this: "I'm not sure who thought it was a good idea to put you on television, but you are the worst I've ever seen. You will NEVER make it in this business. As long as I'm working here, you will not be on the air again. I suggest you go back to your old line of work, and I sure hope you're a better lawyer than you are a reporter."

I gathered the one remaining shred of dignity I had and quickly ran out the door.

The great thing about news stations is that they all have soundproof edit bays. I found one that wasn't being used and proceeded to hide there, crying, for nearly two hours. I called my agent and told her it was okay if she wanted to fire me.

"I'm so humiliated," I sobbed. "What if he's right?"

"He isn't," she replied, talking me off the ledge. "He's crazy and we're going to prove him wrong."

Mr. New Boss gave me the option of continuing to show up for work every day, doing desk work but never appearing in front of the camera. The pay was so low and the humiliation so high, I decided to leave immediately and start looking for another job. As I cleaned out the few things I had at my desk, I heard snickers from the experienced reporters who'd told me I didn't belong.

The experience taught me that nothing is guaranteed,

and that no job is ever going to love you back. It doesn't matter how committed you are, how hard you work, or how good your attitude is—sometimes life doesn't go your way. Finding your self-worth in what you do for a living is a dangerous thing, and getting my heart broken in that very first TV job burned that concept into my heart and soul.

At that point, I only had four months of occasional on-air reporting under my belt. To apply for another TV job, I knew that I needed a lot more on-camera material than a handful of taped segments. So I reached out to the technical crew at my soon-to-be-former station and asked if I could come in on a weekend to record some phony reports and clips of me anchoring. At the time, I still didn't realize how many people that involved and what a big ask it was. Chutzpah! I brought in trays of cookies and treats from a local bakery, and several changes of clothes. For the next hour, I would read a couple of stories, change my jacket, and then tackle a few more. Eventually, I cobbled together enough material for a résumé reel.

My agent started shopping me around, and I scoured the web for any opportunity I could find. No market was too big for my ambitions or too small for my ego. Sheldon and I started to talk about the possibility that we'd probably have to move in order for me to pursue this dream.

"Let's do it," he said enthusiastically. "What have we got to lose?"

But guess what? No one was interested. Days became weeks, weeks became months—and still nothing.

Now the questions really started to close in on me. I'd felt certain the Lord was guiding me down this path, but what if it was just my ego or selfishness? Stations in the smallest markets in the tiniest corners of the country wouldn't return my calls. I spent my days hiding from the friends and family who had questioned my decision to quit my legal career. I could feel them saying, "I told you so," even if they never actually said the words. I began to contemplate returning to the law. It was an honorable profession, but the thought of going back left me demoralized on so many different levels.

In the midst of all the turmoil, I knew there were lessons to be learned. I remember praying only half in jest, *Lord, I know there is meaning and purpose in all this. Could you just go ahead and reveal the deep truths I'm supposed to glean, so I can digest them and we can get this show on the road?* But we all know that's not how it works. So, I waited . . . and waited. I surrendered all my plans and started plotting ways to get back to a steady paycheck.

Just when I was close to giving up, two stations in two very different TV markets—West Palm Beach, Florida, and Charlotte, North Carolina—invited me to come for interviews. As a seventh-generation Floridian whose happy place is the beach, West Palm felt like heaven to me with its sunny weather, sidewalk cafés, and the beach always within reach. The open position was for an evening anchor. I'd never even anchored a single telecast, but that résumé reel of mine sure told a different story!

When Sheldon and I talked about it, though, we realized that the West Palm job would move us even farther away from his tight-knit family. And while I was delighted by the idea of having sunny, hot weather year-round, Sheldon missed having four seasons and wanted a break from the oppressive heat. Before I'd even interviewed in Charlotte, Sheldon made it clear that he hoped that's where we'd land. They had a reporter opening, but by the time I arrived, the bosses had decided they wanted me to do a test with their morning anchor to see if I'd fit as a cohost.

Within days, both stations had put offers on the table. There was no doubt in my mind: we were staying in Florida. The station had offered me a prestigious evening anchor slot. No more exhausting overnight shifts, and the location left no chance that we'd ever be shoveling show. Yet Sheldon was fully convinced our next move would be to Charlotte. We tried to talk about it, but it only erupted into extended arguments that ended in stalemates. At one point, we actually stopped talking to each other. Living under the same roof, wanting two very different things. It's the only time in twenty-three years of marriage that we've been at a total impasse with no compromise in sight. We couldn't live in two different cities, but neither of us wanted to budge.

All my life I'd heard sermons about women submitting to their husbands. I'd also heard many people dismiss that idea as outdated and oppressive. However, I knew the rest of the scripture that went along with that principle: "Husbands, love your wives, just as Christ also loved the church and gave Himself for her." In other words, submission isn't a one-sided deal. Multiple times in that chapter in Ephesians, husbands are commanded to love their wives in a totally selfless, sacrificing way. Men, love your wives. Wives, respect their leadership. Yes, I got it intellectually, but now it was intruding on my real life, and I had to decide what I really believed.

Sheldon is very logical, and he made a strong case for Charlotte. It put us geographically in between both our families. It was a much bigger TV market, a growing city with a lot to offer. If I wanted to keep moving up the ladder in news, the station in Charlotte made more sense as the next step.

I hadn't had a bite in months, so I really needed to take one of these jobs. I called West Palm and said I wouldn't be coming. The boss thought I was playing hardball, though, and responded by offering me more and more money.

"The truth is, my husband and I are at an impasse," I tried to explain. "As much as I want to take this job, I'm not going to blow up my marriage over it, and I believe in letting my husband make the final call."

When I finally told him that nothing he offered would make me take the job, he seemed speechless. He sputtered a bit and finally wished me well.

AS we unpacked boxes and Sheldon interviewed for a new job, I settled in at mine. My greatest joy in working in Charlotte was my fantastic morning coanchor, John Carter. Tall, Southern, and always with a twinkle in his eye, John could spin a yarn and have you in stitches in no time. I was still such a newbie to the business, but he taught me the ropes. Even though our days started around 2:00 a.m., he was always smiling and encouraging the team. A fantastic newswriter, he took on the unofficial role of actually producing the show many times. Every day he showed me the value of hard work and calling everyone around you to a higher level by personal example. I'm not sure he knew what a "project" he was getting when I signed on, but he couldn't have been more gracious.

I started on the morning show and slowly started to take on special assignments, filling in for the evening anchors and reporting live from events like the Republican National Convention in New York. I eventually took one of the evening anchor slots while continuing to report on the street.

One crazy night, I was sent to a massive house fire. As I interviewed the neighbors and gathered what information I could from the fire crews on the scene, I learned the authorities believed it might be a case of arson involving a disgruntled handyman or worker who'd been inside the house. At the very moment I went live on the air, that man showed up on the scene, made some potentially incriminating statements, and the last glimpse I got as I was wrapping up my report was him being taken to a police car. I'd never before had a suspect show up on the scene of a crime and get arrested while I was doing a story about the incident—and it hasn't happened since!

After advancing through several positions in Charlotte, I was anchoring one of the evening shows when a call came from Washington, DC. Would I be interested in anchoring a weekend show there? In a top-ten market? Yes! We'd loved our time in Charlotte, but my three-year contract was coming to an end and we had a decision to make. I went for an interview, but the secrecy was so tight that I didn't actually see the station. A car picked me up from the airport, took me to a lovely Italian restaurant where I ate with the bosses, then I went straight back to the airport for my return flight.

The offer came, we packed up again, and Sheldon found a job at a speaker's bureau in Washington. The new station paired me with a cohost, Eun Yang, who became a lifelong friend. You never know how you'll click with an on-air partner, but we bonded so quickly that we started to drive the studio crew crazy. Her favorite magazine? My favorite magazine. Her favorite TV show? Same as mine. Devoted to Jesus? Yep, that, too. We spent our commercial breaks sharing snacks and celebrity gossip, often in laughing fits that came dangerously close to ending up on air.

One of the reasons I took the weekend job in Washington was because Tim Russert was hosting *Meet the Press* down the hall from where we shot our local Sunday morning broadcast. Every week we tried to casually "run into" the high-profile guests who appeared on Tim's show. From senators to heads of state, they had no idea who we were, but that didn't matter to us. *Meet the Press* also had a luxurious breakfast spread of pastries, juices, and coffees, and we often tried to sneak a taste. One Sunday, we saw that a sign had been posted on the table: FOR NETWORK PERSONNEL AND GUESTS ONLY. Eun and I took that as a personal challenge and continued to snack from the forbidden feast. Eventually, they started locking the door and we were relegated back to the minors.

During those first years in local news, I often felt frustrated, worried that I'd never get the chance to cover the big national stories I found so fascinating. But as I look back on it now, I wouldn't change a thing. I got knocked down many times, but I also made lifelong friends who taught me so much. What I didn't realize then was how much I still had to learn—humility, tenacity, patience—and how much I'd need those skills when the next step finally came.

Dream Job

Fox News Channel launched the year I graduated from law school, on my dad's birthday. Over the years, he became one of the channel's biggest fans. As a staunch conservative, he'd finally found a media outlet that acknowledged his existence rather than mocking or ignoring him. More often than not, if his TV was on, it was on Fox.

As I fought my way through different TV markets, I had been submitting my best work to anyone with connections at Fox News. The network had quickly taken over the cable news ratings, and I knew I would be the perfect fit for them. That is, if I could get them to know I existed. I pressed my agent over and over again to keep trying, but we couldn't get a call or email returned—and certainly not an interview.

When it became clear that the traditional routes wouldn't get me there, Sheldon had an idea. He had booked some speakers at an early morning breakfast event where Brit Hume would be speaking. Brit was then anchoring *Special Report* and overseeing Fox's Washington, DC, bureau.

"Hon, this is the perfect opening," Sheldon said. "Who better than the head of Fox's DC bureau to get a look at your work?"

"I don't know . . . it feels a bit stalkerish," I said. I wasn't sure it would make the best first impression. I'd have to think about it.

The night before, I was anchoring our station's 11:00 p.m. Sunday news show. Because of a sporting event that ran way over time, it wasn't until nearly 1:00 a.m. that we went on for our broadcast. It seemed like I had just gotten home and fallen into bed when Sheldon shook me awake. "Come on, you've got to get up and go meet Brit Hume."

UGH. I felt exhausted, and one look in the mirror revealed a giant zit that had seemingly sprouted up in the middle of my right cheek overnight.

The more he prodded, the less I felt like going. "No, honey, I don't look good or feel great. This isn't the time for me to try to wow anyone." But Sheldon wouldn't take no for an answer. He firmly coaxed me to get into the shower and get going.

When we arrived on-site at the massive Washington Hilton, crowds of convention attendees had already packed the place full. We found the greenroom where the speakers were waiting and learned the program was running behind. That meant Brit was stuck with us for a while, a captive audience. We quickly made introductions and Sheldon boldly pronounced, "Brit, I don't know if you recognize my wife, but she's a local reporter and anchor for NBC here in Washington."

Brit nodded and then asked me, "Well, what do you want to do long term?" The question was so direct, I knew this was one of those moments in life when you have to step up or always regret it.

"I'd love to come work for you at Fox!" I blurted.

Brit chuckled softly and said, "People tell me that all the time, but they just aren't prepared for what we do." He went on to share the story of a substandard résumé reel he'd gotten from one young woman who kept mispronouncing the word *defibrillator.* He gave me his work address, told me to send over some of my work, and then politely made it clear that the conversation was over. Yikes, that was embarrassing.

My giant blemish and I decided to take a walk around the hotel and leave the men to chat. Still, I was proud of myself for sticking my neck out. I'd never have to wonder what could have been if I hadn't been too afraid to speak up.

After pulling myself back together, I went back to the room, and Brit quickly cornered me. "When can you start?" he said.

He was so insistent, I thought it was a joke. I looked at Sheldon in complete bewilderment. I'd only been gone ten minutes—what the heck happened?

Sheldon later told me that when I left the room, Brit casually asked if I liked politics. "Definitely," Sheldon said. "She worked in the Florida legislature when she was in law school, and—"

"She went to law school?" Brit interrupted, seeming intrigued. "Did she finish?"

"She graduated with honors and went on to practice before getting into TV news," Sheldon said.

All of a sudden, Brit became animated. "Do you think she'd want to cover the Supreme Court?" he asked. Megyn Kelly had just left her post covering the court to start a new daytime show in New York with Bill Hemmer. Brit had been searching for someone to take up the legal beat, but he didn't want to interview anyone who hadn't worked as an attorney. By the time I walked back through the door, he was on a mission to hire me.

When Brit asked how soon I could start, I explained that I still had several months left on my contract with NBC. "So not any time soon."

Brit was being called for his speech. "We've gotta figure this out," he said as someone pulled him toward the stage. "Promise you'll be right here when I finish."

I most certainly was. The speech went by in a flash, with the crowd laughing and applauding loudly and often. Sheldon and I were shell-shocked by the conversation we'd just had.

When he came off the stage, Brit asked me and Sheldon to walk with him as he made a beeline to the car waiting to take him to work. Again, he asked when I could start. I reminded him that I was under contract and he insisted we'd figure out a way to settle that. He needed someone on the legal beat immediately.

As soon as Sheldon and I got home, I called my agent to relay the startling good news. We arranged to get samples of my work over to Brit so he could share them with the New York bosses as well. Weeks went by and nothing happened. I was anxious and excited, and then disappointed that this didn't seem to be going anywhere. Then seemingly out of the blue, I got a call that Roger Ailes wanted to meet with me. Within days I was on a train, trying to download Roger's book, *You Are the Message*, into my brain on the three-hour ride.

The wait for the interview felt endless. At the time, the second floor was an antiseptic place with dated flooring and paint. I knew Ailes was a busy man, but I couldn't tell if this was also a test—icing the kicker, as it were. I went to the restroom and gave myself a pep talk in the mirror. "You have come this far, and none of this is by chance. Remember that you are smart and educated and you've always known you'd be perfect for Fox."

By the time an assistant called me into Roger's office, my nerves were under control. Walls of windows let light into the room. Another wall was covered with multiple TVs tracking what every network on the spectrum was up to.

Roger put his hand out and greeted me. "I've heard a lot about you from Brit."

Our chat seemed to last forever. We talked about love of our country, and my brother's military service. I was surprised that the head of a channel would have so much time to devote to a random local reporter, but I was determined to stay and make my case for as long as he'd listen. He finally said, "Well, they're going to crucify me if I hire another blond lawyer," chuckling to himself as if he enjoyed the criticism.

It was difficult to gauge how well I'd been received, but I headed back to "real" life with the peace of knowing I'd at least gotten my shot. Weeks passed, and no job offer came. More weeks passed, still with no word.

One day, just as I was preparing to go live from a fire at an apartment complex, my phone rang. Normally, I'd ignore it—but it was my agent calling again and again. When I picked up, her voice sounded urgent. Fox needed me to start at the Supreme Court right away. "If you don't make yourself available, they're going to hire someone else," she said.

I was still under contract with NBC and not yet in a period where I could actually entertain an offer from anyone. I had considered my options: asking NBC for permission to negotiate an offer elsewhere or convincing Fox to wait for a few more months.

I went to my bosses at NBC, asking them whether they thought there was an opportunity for me to move to the network level. If not, I wanted their permission to look at other offers. The conversation didn't go well. The message was clear: they wanted me to stay in my current position, and no—I could not start negotiating elsewhere. I felt trapped. NBC wasn't considering promoting me, but they also wouldn't let me seek that opportunity somewhere else. They were in the right. I had signed a contract and I would honor it.

My agent relayed the news back to Fox, and they let us know they'd be moving on. I felt so conflicted. I prayed, *How could you lead me to Brit and to this opening, and then slam the door shut?* I struggled with the decision to keep from going behind NBC's back. Almost everyone I knew in the industry had said, "Everyone does business this way. Negotiate your deal with Fox now, work out all the terms, and then sign it the day you leave NBC." Boy, was that tempting. But it just didn't sit right with me or Sheldon. If God was in this, we'd have to trust Him to guide us around the obstacles.

My best friend, Ina, came to town and we attended a women's conference that weekend in DC. She knew the internal conflict I was struggling with, and how many years I'd been trying to get anyone at Fox to give me a shot. Between sessions, we walked around the arena where all the speakers had their books on display. I replayed all the conversations and options to her yet again, when suddenly we turned a corner. I looked up and saw a massive display of a book titled *When I Lay My Isaac Down*. I knew what I had to do.

Growing up, I'd heard and read the story of Abraham and Isaac too many times to count. After a lifetime of promises from God that his descendants would number more than the stars and sand, Abraham and Sarah had finally been blessed with a son of their own. This had been a long time coming; Abraham was one hundred and Sarah wasn't far behind! But later, in Genesis 22, God tests Abraham by asking him to sacrifice Isaac. As anguished as he is by every step, Abraham moves forward in faith. Just as he is about to follow through, an angel stops him and says, "Now I know that you fear God, because you have not withheld from me your son . . ."

That job at Fox had become my Isaac. In much less dramatic fashion I knew what I was being asked to do: let it go and trust the Lord for the rest. I wasn't letting it go with the assurance that I would be given the job—just like Abraham didn't take Isaac to the altar fully expecting that God would stop him at the last minute. I was releasing it for good, trusting that God had a better plan than the one I'd been dreaming of.

Sheldon and I talked it over, and let my agent know I wouldn't be doing a secret deal with Fox before I was legally permitted to do so. Both my agent and I knew the risk I was taking, but she'd known Sheldon and me long enough to respect our position.

A few days later, Sheldon got a call at work. "Brit Hume on the line for you."

"I know I can't negotiate a contract with your wife," Brit started. "But hypothetically, if we offered her the Supreme Court job when her deal is up with NBC, do you think she'd come work for us?"

"I can't speak for her," Sheldon said, considering his words carefully. "But my gut says yes."

"That's all I wanted to know," Brit said. And then he hung up.

Weeks later, I entered a window in which I was allowed to entertain offers from outside. Any offer would be presented to NBC, and if the network decided to match it, I would have to stay at NBC. But when Fox put together a package that was a major step up from where I was at NBC, including a national position that would finally get me off weekend duty, NBC balked. One of my bosses actually said to my agent, "I just don't see it. She doesn't have what it takes to be a national correspondent." Once again, I was determined to prove a boss who didn't believe in me wrong. I started planning my move to Fox just after Thanksgiving 2007.

I remember arriving on day one and going through the formalities of getting my security badge picture taken. The photo wasn't exactly flattering, but I was thrilled to have that piece of plastic proving I finally worked there. I quickly learned that Fox was a sink-or-swim operation. There was no welcoming party, no formal training on the software systems. It was simply, "Here's your desk. Get to work."

I was used to pitching stories, chasing interviews, and putting together at least one piece a day. But this was like walking up to a whirling carousel and struggling to find a place to jump on. Thank God for my good friend Molly Henneberg, whom I'd known before getting to Fox. She was my lifeline. Every hour of the day has a different producer and different vibe. For what seemed like months, all the producers in New York had no idea who I was. It was a byzantine maze of people and personalities, and I wasn't sure where I fit in.

I slowly learned that if I didn't pitch stories of my own, I'd be assigned to any number of rabbit trails to chase. Sometimes they panned out, sometimes they didn't. And even when you think you've got an interesting story, convincing the producers and getting a two-minute slot on their show takes effort. It wasn't like local news, where I was expected to chase a story and be on the air every day—often for multiple shows. No, I learned that at the national level there are way more correspondents than there are slots for airtime. That meant constantly hustling to break news or own a big story. Otherwise you spent the day at your desk trying to look busy but feeling invisible.

Every job has its challenges, and my new position at Fox was no exception. Reporters from other stations were covering my beat, but most of them had been there for years, and had no interest in helping the newbie from Fox. But I loved the intellectual challenge of covering Washington: digging into policy and working to build sources without coming across as too aggressive. It was one thing to get someone's business card, but the goal was to gain their trust enough to know their personal cell number.

Yet I realized there would always be so much more to the job than simply reporting. Competition was tough both internally and externally, and breaking out of the pack of talented correspondents was a serious challenge. There were many polished, smart people on our bench. Getting called into the game on a big story or event was one of the only ways to know if the bosses thought you had something extra. Every time I got tapped for a live report, I immediately called or texted my parents so they could watch. Often, I was bumped by more important news. But for the first time in my career, my dad could see my work on live TV and he told me how proud he felt.

Grateful to be at Fox, but still finding my footing, I was thrown another curveball. We had some changes in personnel and the bosses were scrambling to fill the weekend reporting slots. Since I was the newest hire, they told me I'd be reassigned to a Wednesday-to-Sunday schedule. Though I'd been hired for a Monday-through-Friday job, there was no language in my contract guaranteeing those days. (Big. Lesson. Learned.) The DC bureau needed weekend coverage, and I was the obvious candidate. Sheldon and I had finally gotten our weekends back, and here I was feeling like I was back to square one: fighting to get airtime and relegated once again to weekends.

Discouraged, but believing I was exactly where God wanted

me to be, I tried to make the best of the situation. I did get more airtime on the weekends, and that experience helped me improve my skills: quickly digesting information, turning multiple scripts for all the different shows, and doing it all while managing the nerves of speaking on live television. We fell into a rhythm that allowed me to work weekend mornings and to attend church on Saturday nights. I felt lonely on Mondays and Tuesdays because all my friends were working or busy with their children. Sheldon and I didn't have a single day off together, and I often wondered how long we could sustain that.

In yet another unexpected twist, one of the weekend anchors left and the bosses asked if I'd like to give it a try. I knew it would be a bit different from what I had done at the local level, but I'd been anchoring for years and I was thrilled at the opportunity.

The one thing I always dreaded as a local anchor was when a segment involved a guest. You never knew what they were going to blurt out, or where the conversation would go. I preferred reading scripts I had edited and proofed multiple times before going on the air. Well, that's not how most Fox shows work. Not only do we have live guests, they often get paired up for heated debates on topics as wide-ranging as pot legalization, congressional budgets, or the future of NASA. I'd have to develop a new skill.

The wardrobe was also very different. I felt most comfortable when dressed in the suits I'd worn in the courtroom years ago. Now I was being sent options from our wardrobe department that felt more like the ones from my pageant days: colorful and fitted. I tried to find the happy medium and focus on the content I needed to digest. I floundered a bit in those early days of anchoring at Fox. Everyone had an opinion on my hair, my clothes, the questions I asked—or didn't. It made me second-guess my every move. I was so nervous and overly sensitive to the criticism coming from all sides. I lost that weekend anchor slot more than once.

Social media was now a full-fledged part of the news conversation, and I often checked to see what people thought of my performance. The reviews were often mixed. "Who thought this chick should be hosting a show?" some people said. Others shot back, "She's a rising star." When I find myself paying attention to these opinions, it's a reminder that I've started finding my worth in all the wrong places. It's easy to do in this business, but it's a critical wrong turn.

As I regained my bearings, I started advocating more for myself and the stories I wanted to cover. I was building sources at the Supreme Court and breaking a bit of news here and there. I'd been at Fox for years when I got a call one afternoon. "We need you to come to New York tonight so you can fill in for Megyn Kelly tomorrow." At the time, she was paired up with Bill Hemmer in the highly rated 9:00–11:00 a.m. show. I was elated that they would ask and felt completely unprepared to accept. But there was no question; I had to go.

I remember feeling sensitive about my weight at the time. The women in our New York bureau seemed so skinny and flawless. Their streamlined, bright dresses stood in contrast to the navy and gray suits I often wore while on the legal beat. I tried to pick out an outfit that would both hide my body and be slightly more colorful. It didn't work. I got an email from the wardrobe department after the show saying that my outfit wasn't "quite right." Bulky tweed jackets weren't the look of daytime television. I knew I would have to come out of my shell a bit if I wanted to get invited back.

The invitations to New York kept coming, and that's when I started meeting with Ailes on a somewhat regular basis. His language was often coarse and bawdy, and I tried to politely laugh away my discomfort with some of his conversation topics and vocabulary. He asked me to speculate about people's sexuality and their bodies. This man was the final word for on-air talent at Fox; there was no other decision maker. When it came to your airtime and chances for promotion, Ailes was the be-all and end-all.

Having worked on sexual harassment cases as an attorney, I knew what my legal options were with respect to the uncomfortable environment Ailes's meetings put me in—at least on paper. But how that translates in real life is complex. The law would require me to show that I had reported the trouble to our internal Human Resources Department, but it felt like Ailes had a choke hold on the entire company. I couldn't imagine reporting him to anyone on the inside. I decided my only option—if I wanted to keep my dream job—was to keep my mouth shut.

Because I was based in the DC bureau, I didn't have deep friendships with any of the New York women. I was anxious to figure out if other female coworkers were having these same interactions with Ailes, suggestive conversations and wildly inappropriate questions. I finally began to make some headway and heard stories about him spotting someone on the air and calling them to his office so he could see their outfits in person, asking them to twirl around and give him a full 360-degree view. As I got linked into the chatter network, I found many of the woman at Fox were uncomfortable in these meetings with Ailes, but they felt it was the cost of doing business. Laugh along, extricate yourself when you can, and never let him think you've been offended.

For years, that was my strategy, but I finally hit a wall. On one particular occasion, he called me in two days in a row. He always commented on how physically attractive he thought I was, but then he would say I was too uptight, and it was a turnoff to men. He said I needed to work on making sure people thought that if I went out on a date, I could "be a good time." He suggested I find more camera options for showing off my body, explaining that one anchor had gotten "smart" about using a standing position to show her figure from behind. The innuendo never let up and there was a bottom line: I needed to prove I could be sexier both personally and professionally.

The sad thing is, I actually tried to comply with this directive. Several times, I wore outfits that were too provocative for a serious journalist. I tried working flirtatious language into shows that were supposed to be hard news programs. When I think about it now, I cringe. Why was I so willing to put myself in this position, demeaning my integrity in the hopes one man would take notice and give me his approval?

I would never even entertain acting this way in my private life. Why was I willing to do it professionally?

The truth is, I had my eyes on the wrong prize. I was desperate to win the approval of a man I knew could make or break reporters and anchors. I had thrown so much of myself into my job, it had become an idol—even beyond the situation with Ailes. I would break plans last minute to stay late at the office. I said yes to assignments I absolutely did not want to do and generally became a doormat. I'm not talking about times when there's substantive breaking news, when everyone in the office pitches in happily for weeks or months, whatever it takes. I'm talking about having no boundaries when it came to any request that might even minimally advance me at Fox. No matter where you work, that's not a healthy place to be.

My faith tells me this: I am the daughter of a king. God loves me unconditionally, and He wants my undivided attention. He will never abandon or betray me, and He also expects me to live a life set apart. Slowly, I had allowed Ailes to push his way onto the throne of my life. It had to stop.

Then, in the summer of 2014, Ailes said the words I had been longing to hear: "You deserve your own show." Just when I had decided I couldn't play the game anymore, he sucked me back in. I put together a presentation outlining my ideas for an original show, along with hard ratings data from when I filled in for anchors like Chris Wallace and Megyn Kelly. I worked for hours on the graphics, organized the documents, and tucked them into a bright red folder.

As I walked into Ailes's office to discuss my pitch, I did so with trepidation. I handed him a copy of the materials and told him I'd love to walk him through what I'd prepared. But he tossed the red folder aside and told me that wouldn't be necessary.

Instead, he asked me, "So whose show should I take away?" Ailes constantly preached loyalty, so the question didn't sit right with me. (I would learn later that this was a tactic he often used to test whether a reporter or anchor could be pressured to turn on a coworker.) I took the high road, spitting out something about hoping that if something wonderful happened to a current anchor—like winning the lottery—I was prepared to launch my show.

But as the conversation wandered once again into familiar territory, it became clear that Ailes wasn't serious about me getting a show. He was never going to look inside that red folder. I decided right then and there that the dance was over. I needed to pick up whatever shreds of dignity I had left, walk out of that office, and never return. As I left that day, I made peace with the consequences of that decision. Shutting out Ailes wasn't going to move me up the ladder, but it was the only way to restore the integrity I had sacrificed trying to get his attention.

I never met with him again, but when Gretchen Carlson made her now-famous claims two years later, several of us with similar experiences found one another and shared our stories. I avoided speaking about the issue publicly because it felt like a no-win situation. Roger clearly had positive qualities, and I knew the many stories of his kindness to Fox employees and contributors in tragic times of need. It was a pressure-packed, confusing time.

Even as the story picked up steam, it didn't seem possible that Ailes wouldn't triumph and stay firmly ensconced in his powerful position. I just wanted to keep my head down and do my work. We were in the midst of the 2016 national RNC and DNC conventions, and our phones rang nonstop as the other networks and newspapers dug into what happened. Somehow the *New York Times* even got my personal cell-phone number.

When it became clear Ailes actually was leaving Fox, I breathed my first sigh of relief in weeks. And then I started to hear more women's stories. Some of them will never be publicly known, and I can't speak to the veracity of each one. I do know this: the allegations were widespread and very much consistent with what I myself knew to be true about his behavior.

The events launched a national conversation about how we can address workplace rules that leave many employees feeling like they have no good options. There's been tremendous change at Fox, and as a woman in America, I feel like there's still much work left to do. But in the end, I learned that no earthly goal or success is worth feeling like I've sold my soul to get it.

Better Vision

Like most people, I like to think that I can grow and deepen as a person when things are going well. But if I'm being honest with myself, I've yet to achieve that kind of maturity on a consistent basis. The truth is, the worst circumstances are where I learn and stretch the most. Life is cyclical, and I love the periods of rest and sunshine. But guess what? While we all need those blissful, mountaintop seasons, those experiences aren't usually where we grow beyond ourselves. So, though I don't enjoy pain, I do understand the purpose that comes when we are called to live through difficult times.

I've always been fascinated by 2 Corinthians 12, the passage in which the Apostle Paul talks about his "thorn in the flesh" and how God refused to remove it after Paul asked three times. Instead, Paul was left to wrestle with the reality of living with whatever it was that tortured him so much. Was it physical pain? Emotional distress? Theologians have debated that for ages. All I know is that it clearly troubled him deeply, and relief wasn't in the divine plan.

Yet when Paul embraces God's message to him, "My grace is sufficient for you, for my power is made perfect in weakness," he decides that he will "boast" in his weaknesses, even to the point of "delighting" in hardships, persecutions, and difficulties. "When I am weak, then I am strong," he writes.

Growing up, I'd read those verses and heard countless sermons about them, but it wasn't until recently, when I went through a period of enormous pain, both physical and emotional, that I fully grasped the truth and beauty in that passage.

It all started shortly before my fortieth birthday. As I was sleeping one night, I suddenly bolted upright as searing pain ripped through one of my eyes. It felt sort of like a time, years earlier, when I'd scratched my cornea with a hairbrush, but this time there was no clear cause. I'd merely been asleep. I got up and stumbled to the bathroom, looking for eye drops or anything to relieve the excruciating pain. Hours later, when the pain finally subsided to a manageable level, I drifted off to sleep shortly before my alarm went off. How strange.

Several days later, it happened again. My face was flooded with tears as my eye swelled to a puffy, painful mess. I tried a hot compress, but that only seemed to make things worse. I stumbled off to work the next day with double vision in the damaged eye and called my optometrist to see how quickly I could get an appointment.

Having handled my contact and glasses prescriptions for years, he counseled me that I was heading into an age group where dry eye could become a real problem. He sent me away with some drops, which I applied religiously, but the problem struck again and again over the next few weeks—and now in both eyes. Something was going on. I needed help.

I searched out a well-respected ophthalmologist and traveled forty-five minutes to see him at the first available appointment. He too noted the dryness I was experiencing and suggested that I was probably wearing my contacts too much. But in my experience, the converse seemed to be true. I told him that the only time I seemed to have a bit of success in avoiding the nighttime pain was when I slept with my extended-wear contacts *in*. I didn't know why it seemed to work, just that it did. And oddly enough, I had zero problems during the day.

"You really can't wear your contacts overnight," he cautioned, "and you should try wearing your glasses more during the day." That seemed reasonable. He also suggested some heavier over-the-counter drops and put me on a prescription specifically designed for chronic dry eyes.

Still, in the coming weeks, the episodes only grew more frequent and more painful. It had been months since this started and the hopelessness was starting to creep in. I was exhausted, but increasingly fearful of falling asleep. I felt like one of the kids in a Freddy Krueger movie: desperate for sleep, but knowing there was a monster waiting for them if they dozed off. There were a growing number of days that I headed in to work with not only double vision, but also pounding migraines that seemed to be triggered by the eye injuries. I now carried drops with me everywhere I went, including the shower.

I returned to the second doctor again, now desperate. The pain had grown so intense, it often made me throw up. Crying and terrified, I would huddle on the floor of the bathroom in the dark of night, sick to my stomach and begging

God to rescue me. Often my prayers were just whispered over and over, "God, please help me." The only words I could croak out.

On that visit, I tried to urgently and firmly convey the situation to my doctor.

"The pain has gotten nearly unbearable," I told him, choking back tears while trying to convey how critical the situation had become. "I'm truly at the end of my rope."

But despite my plea, I could tell he wasn't getting it. He said to me, "I think you're just really emotional." Stunned. Silence.

You better believe I was emotional! Over the last year, my life had morphed into an endless cycle of indescribable pain and crippling exhaustion. I gathered my things and vowed never to return to that office. I was barely holding it together at that point, and the doctor's inability to throw me a lifeline was crushing.

For the next few months, I refused to seek out another doctor, instead scouring the internet to figure out what was happening to me. Sheldon was the only person who had even a clue about what was going on with me. I didn't tell friends, family, or coworkers much—if anything. There were no words, no diagnosis, nothing but a doctor questioning my sanity. Maybe I was losing it. It certainly felt that way.

A word to the wise: never surf the web to diagnose a medical condition. It only takes one minute of searching to find out you have roughly seventeen seconds to live. But I didn't feel like I had any other options at this point, so I poured myself into search engines, medical journals, message boards—anything that provided even the smallest lead. I stumbled into one particular online community of people who had stories just like mine. They wrote of spending hours in emergency rooms in mind-numbing pain, only to be turned away with no information and no relief. Many of them had given up, even to the point where they'd considered taking their own lives.

I totally got it. When you live with chronic pain, the world around you just looks different. You become deadened to almost everything. There is no joy. No joke is funny. No sunset is beautiful. Nothing tastes good. There is no exotic destination you hope to one day visit. You just want everything to stop—to go away.

My life felt completely meaningless. What was the purpose of hanging by a thread in constant torment? Forget living another forty years like this, there were days I couldn't figure out how I would get through the next forty seconds. From the outside, I looked like a successful journalist with a comfortable life, wonderful friends, and a saint of a husband—but on the inside, I started to contemplate what it would look like to leave all that behind. What a relief it would be to escape this cycle of despair and torture. My friends and family might be shocked at first, I reasoned, but they'd forgive me when they discovered the hell I'd been in for the last two years. It pains me to admit that I actually started to think through the logistics of it all.

Through all this, I'd never stopped praying or seeking God. In fact, I believed He'd understand too. My Heavenly Father could see what a deep, black hole I'd tumbled into.

Lord, you above anyone know the truth of this pit I'm living in. I have reached my limit as a human being. I beg you to let me go to sleep and wake up with you.

But all of a sudden, the fact that I no longer thought of suicide as shocking somehow woke me up. I decided I had to level with Sheldon about my internal deliberations. I remember sitting on our bed sobbing.

"I really can't do this any longer," I choked out. "I've been reading online forums . . . people with my same symptoms . . . talking about ending it all . . . and I think I understand that."

The guilt had weighed on me so heavily, but Sheldon received my confession with no judgment. "Shan, we're going to find an answer and I'm going to fight right beside you," he said. He vowed to travel the world and spend every penny we had if that's what it took to find a doctor who would take me seriously and finally diagnose my condition.

That night, Sheldon and I began a new prayer. "Lord, if you choose not to heal me, please just give me someone who can help me through this." I had been so demoralized by the last doctor I'd seen, it scared me to think about finding someone new and communicating just how bad things had gotten without dissolving into a pile of hysterical tears. With Sheldon's help, I found the resolve to try again.

My search led to a cornea specialist right here in DC who'd gotten glowing recommendations. He hadn't been on my insurance plan when I last looked through the database, but we weren't worried about cost at this point. I tentatively called his office, willing myself to keep it together. As best I could, I explained what I was experiencing and asked how quickly I could see the doctor. The receptionist was kind and asked if I could hold. She quickly returned, told me there had been a cancellation, and asked if I could come the next day. "Absolutely!" I said. That night I prayed the Lord would get me through one more night. Just one.

The following day I was scheduled to fill in for Bret Baier on his 6:00 p.m. broadcast of *Special Report*. The doctor's office wasn't too far away, so I went over midday for a check. The medical assistant patiently walked through my history and time line, taking detailed notes.

Not long after, the doctor appeared. Without taking a look at my eyes, he said, "I think I know what you have." *Whoa*.

The doctor explained that my corneas were literally being torn apart every night while I slept. So when I described the pain as feeling like a knife being scraped across my eyeball—that's almost exactly what was happening. Turns out, I have a genetic condition in which the cells of the cornea don't root firmly back into the eyeball. Instead, they are prone to tear off. As I slept and my eye dried out, the surface of the cornea would actually adhere to my eyelid, and then tear when my eyeball moved again.

"I'm 95 percent sure this is what you have," the doctor said. "But let me do the exam and let's see."

I couldn't believe it. Finally, an answer. This man had listened to me and he was going to help. As we talked for several more minutes, I became even more aware that I'd been living with a giant boulder on my back. It was almost a foreign sensation—this new feeling of happiness. That is, until the doctor said six words that brought it all crashing down.

"You should know," he said, pausing to take a breath, "there's no cure." He went on with his explanation and the exam, but I didn't hear anything else he said that day. My mind was racing. How quickly could I get to my car and drive it off a bridge? This couldn't be happening.

Sheldon had been anxiously awaiting my call, but I couldn't even breathe—much less string together a sentence. I don't remember checking out of the office or anything else until I got to my car. I had to go back to the office and get ready for the show. Everyone was waiting for me. It seemed impossible. Tears gushed and I sobbed to the point of hysteria. *God, please. How can this be? I can't go on.*

I'm not someone who thinks I've audibly heard the voice of God, but I do know something happened in that moment of sheer and utter despair. I felt Him say in my spirit, unmistakably: "I will be with you." Not "I will heal you" or "I will take this pain away." Simply: "I will be with you." Those words washed over me like a calming force. Somehow, as I sat in my car in total desolation, I knew God had heard me and was reaching down from heaven to comfort His terrified, exhausted, hopeless child. It would be enough.

When I followed up with my doctor, I quickly learned that although my underlying condition would never go away, there was a range of treatment options—from the insertion of tiny plugs into the tear ducts to large doses of fish oil, using humidifiers, or applying a heavy ointment to coat the eyeballs each night. I started to find relief. It took a while, but I slowly built up to several hours of sleep without overwhelming anxiety that my next cornea tear was waiting just around the corner. Sometimes, the tears did still come. But now I had tools to help manage them. I was no longer completely without hope.

All during this time, the song "Blessings" by Laura Story was playing on the radio. Though I felt like I'd heard it hundreds of times, the lyrics suddenly stopped me in my tracks one day. "What if your blessings come through raindrops, what if your healing comes through tears? What if a thousand sleepless nights are what it takes to know you're near?" I'd had plenty of tears AND sleepless nights. And yet I felt the presence of God. I knew He was sustaining me in a way I might never have experienced if I hadn't spent so much time in that dark valley.

My doctor warned me that my condition would likely worsen with age, and I would probably have to consider surgery at some point. There were no guarantees, he said, but the surgery had been very helpful for most patients with my condition.

The operation would require me to stay away from work for a period of recovery, so for years I continued to put it off. Occasionally, I'd go through a rough patch of tears (usually while traveling in cold, dry climates) and begin thinking seriously about the surgery again. But then I'd head into another campaign cycle or other all-consuming assignment that made it impossible to take a substantial break. Each year my doctor would reintroduce the conversation. "You should really start making plans for this. Your eyes are only getting worse."

I knew he was right, but I just couldn't commit. What if I went through all that and I was a case that didn't work? I sought second, and third, opinions and weighed the pros and cons. But in the fall of 2017, I finally decided to take the plunge.

My bosses at Fox had tapped me to launch a new hard news program at 11:00 p.m. As we worked to put the show together—hiring personnel, working on the show concept, and starting rehearsal—there would be a three- or four-week period where I wouldn't have to be on camera. It seemed like I finally had a window for the operation. I could take a few days off, have the surgery, and then continue to work from home as my eyes recovered. Most everything I'd read or been told said that my eyesight (which, as a side benefit, could be corrected during the operation) would pretty much stabilize within two to three weeks. Perfect!

The procedure wouldn't take long, but I'd have to be awake and fully cooperative as they directed me through it. I had prayed through this and felt so calm on the day of surgery that I turned down the antianxiety medication the nurse offered me. I'd basically be having the surface of my eyeballs taken off, and the surgeon warned me the pain would be intense for the first couple of days.

I left that day with blurry vision and very detailed instructions about all the various eye drops and pain medications the doctors had given me. I knew I wouldn't be able to read during the early stage of my recovery, so I'd downloaded some books on tape and prepared for the worst.

When the medication numbing my eyeballs wore off, I suddenly wished I could turn back the clock and undo this whole thing. As unbearable as the cornea tears had been, the pain following surgery was exponentially worse. The entire surface of both eyeballs had literally been ripped apart. If there was even a sliver of light in the room, prying my eyes open was impossible. I struggled even to open my eyes so that I could get the drops in, but there was a strict schedule and order to things, and I was determined to do it by the book.

I remember Sheldon taking me into our bathroom and literally holding a thick towel over the small window so I could try to get the tiniest opening for the drops. The doctor required a visit to his office within twenty-four hours of surgery and I could not fathom how that was going to happen. I couldn't even pretend to take a shower.

Sheldon managed to get me into comfy black sweats and a matching jacket. I could barely stand up and I certainly couldn't look around to find my way. We decided to call an Uber and I wore my sleeping mask over my matted, dirty hair. Shel led me to the car and I collapsed in pain in the backseat. As the driver took off, the combination of heavy medication and my inability to see where we were going made me instantly carsick.

When we arrived at the office, the nurse quickly took us to an exam room to wait. "I'll need to take a look at your eyes and see how you're progressing," she said. I barely had the strength to respond, and I knew how nonsensical I probably sounded.

"Ma'am, I literally cannot pry my eyes open. The pain

is a solid ten, and I can't control the reflexes keeping them completely closed." Even with my lids shut, the light in the room was unbearable.

The nurse finally came up with a plan to lower the lights and pull open my lower lid so she could drop in some numbing medication. It worked. For a few minutes, I could function again. I explained to the nurse that I'd been taking my medication right on schedule, but it didn't seem to help the searing, throbbing pain. I knew I needed to be eating along with those medications, and Lord knows Sheldon tried, but I couldn't keep much down beyond a bite or two of plain rice.

The doctor seemed shocked when he walked in and saw my disheveled state. I had zero vanity. I just needed to know that things were going to get better—and quick! He did the basic exam and said he'd see me again in a couple of days.

Suddenly, though, I knew I had to get out of there. My stomach, empty of nearly anything but pain medication, was turning upside down. I bolted up and asked someone to lead me to the nearest bathroom. The nurse grabbed my hand and got me there just in time for me to fall to the floor and lose what little there was in my stomach.

Lord, why did I do this? I prayed. *Was this a huge mistake?* Sheldon waited patiently outside the door, then helped me to pull myself together and walk outside to another Uber. Yup, in my puke-stained sweats and sleeping mask. I could not have possibly cared less. I just wanted my next round of pain meds.

Months later an Uber driver who picked me up for a quick trip said, "You know, I was the one who drove you when you were crazy sick and worried you were going to throw up in my car. I think I was taking you and your husband to a doctor appointment." I was mortified, but he said he was glad to see I was back on my feet.

I had numerous follow-up appointments in the days and weeks after surgery, and each time they checked my vision. "Let's see how much you've progressed," they'd say in an upbeat tone. It seemed ludicrous because everything was just blobs and blurs. The medical assistants always seemed a bit worried that nothing was improving from visit to visit. "Well . . ." they'd trail off after the exam was finished, clearly not at liberty to give their own personal assessments of what I feared was true.

I had become panicked. Clearly I was healing at nowhere near the average pace. Each day I would sit for hours in our sunroom, where I read and pray every morning. I'd alternate looking outside and over to the bookcase, to see if I could distinguish anything—trees, book titles, or pictures on the shelf. Almost nothing.

I hated being dependent on other people, but what choice did I have? I couldn't drive, distinguish people's faces, or even read much of anything. How in the world was I going to launch a national TV show in just a couple of weeks? I didn't want my bosses to know how badly I was doing, so I stumbled around the office and kept my head down. It was embarrassing not to be able to greet people in the hallways because I couldn't see who they were. I quit running on the trail by our house because I was too frightened to venture out alone. This was starting to feel like a colossally bad decision.

By then, the pain had mostly subsided, but I had no idea how I was going to pull things together. There was no way I could hide it from the studio crew. "Guys, I gotta be honest," I finally confessed. "I really can't see much and I'm going to need your help." They are an amazing bunch. They adjusted the teleprompter to the largest font size possible and moved the cameras as close to me as they could get. It was a stretch, and I would have to do plenty of ad-libbing when we went on air, but it was the best we could all do. Every commercial break I would apply the thick, gel-based eye drops the doctors had given me, then try to clear up the havoc they were wreaking on my heavy TV makeup.

Not long after the show launched, with my vision still as blurry as ever, we were covering a live event of President Trump visiting Pearl Harbor. Normally as an anchor, you have a rough time line of what will happen—when the president will arrive, who will greet him, where he'll stop along the way. You simply talk viewers through things as you watch them unfold on-screen. The problem was, I couldn't see the TVs in my studio. As much as I'd been able to fake the past few weeks, the game was over. Thank the Lord my colleague Martha MacCallum was on the ground in Hawaii for the president's visit. I kept tossing back to her whenever it was clear I couldn't see what was happening. That tap dance got us through, but it made me realize how much trouble I was in. If my vision didn't improve, there was no way I could do this job long term.

I pestered my doctor, probing for answers about why my vision hadn't improved. I was under enormous pressure with the launch of the new show, and the unforeseen complications with my vision were driving me to my limits. Later that night, sitting on a comfy couch in my church counselor's office, I sobbed and unloaded everything I'd been hiding from my coworkers.

"This entire show is on my back, and I'm not even functioning at a basic level," I said. "I can't even tell my bosses how bad it is. So, it's not only my impaired vision, it's managing the secrecy, too."

The timing felt horrible, but my counselor disagreed. She knows I hate being dependent on anyone else. Just ask my mom—she'll tell you how fiercely independent I've been since exiting the womb.

"Shannon, I know how much you hate the idea of being vulnerable, but you're left no choice," my counselor said. "That may be the purpose of this entire trial—leaning on God, your friends, your coworkers. You cannot do this alone." In other words, putting on a happy face wasn't going to help anyone. It was time to come clean.

So I started with a post on social media. "I've always thought of being dependent and vulnerable as highly undesirable," I wrote, "but I've been learning how egotistical that is. We aren't supposed to be self-sufficient robots." I laid bare my emotions and fears and told the truth about where I was in the recovery process. I knew I was in this place for a reason.

It was one thing to make myself vulnerable from the remove of social media, but another thing altogether to do it in person. For months, I'd been scheduled to speak at a gathering at the Cove, a retreat center outside Asheville, North Carolina. I'd been invited to talk about journalism and my faith, but I did NOT want to do either. How could I stand up in front of an audience that I couldn't even see and talk about my awesome life?

As I poured out my heart to Sheldon he said, "Don't try to act like everything's perfect. You can be honest about the fact that you're struggling." So that's what I decided to do. My mom agreed to meet me in North Carolina and act as my "seeing-eye human" for the weekend.

Navigating the airport nearly left me in tears. I developed a deep empathy for people who need assistance to do just about anything. All the signs telling me where to go were blurry messes of fuzzy, illegible shapes. I walked slowly, embarrassed that I couldn't maintain my usual breakneck pace of getting from point A to point B. I worried that people were staring at me. What if they recognized me from TV and wondered why I looked aimless and confused? How would I find the kind gentleman the retreat center had sent to pick me up?

When I arrived at the auditorium, the feeling of vulnerability was amplified. I think one of the hosts thought I was kidding when I asked her not to get too far ahead of me as we walked, since I couldn't see much without her guidance. Everyone was incredibly kind. These were people of faith who would be understanding in the midst of my struggle. So instead of taking to the stage and telling them how excited I was about the new show, I told the truth. I told them I couldn't see their faces or the big clock on the back wall that was supposed to tell me when to stop talking. I told them I was discouraged and frightened, but that I knew the Lord was calling me to lean back into Him like never before. I quoted 2 Corinthians and talked about how my weakness made me strong because it forced me to quit relying on myself and turn my focus toward heaven. Honesty. That was all I had to give.

The response was overwhelming. I stayed for more than an hour talking to folks who had lined up to share their stories with me, and to offer prayers and encouragement. "Thank you for sharing your pain; I'm struggling, too," some said. Many others told me, "Now I know exactly how to pray for you." The people I met that weekend may never realize how much they sustained me through that trying time. Had I tried to play it cool, I would have missed the huge blessing of their kindness.

Mom and I decided she should come back to DC with me, since Sheldon was on a weeklong trip. I took her with me when I went to interview Vice President Pence. I've navigated the US Capitol hundreds of times, ever since I worked there as an intern back in the 1990s, but that day was tough. I still couldn't see much, and everything was starting to run together. We had cleared all security requirements for my mom to join me, yet something had come up on the Hill that day and they blocked her at one checkpoint. My frustrations began to boil over. It wasn't my finest hour. After much wrangling and many delays, both of us were finally let into the interview. But when I saw how much it meant to my mother to meet the vice president, and how kind he was to her, I felt guilty about how short my fuse had become.

"Mr. Vice President, it is an honor to meet you," my mom

said with tears in her eyes. She had promised her friends in Tallahassee that she'd tell him they were all praying for the Pence family.

"That means so much to us," he said as he shook her hand.

It was clear I still had plenty of learning and growing to do. I wish I could say I've been a model of patience and faith ever since then, but who am I fooling? I did begin to settle into a much deeper dependence on the Lord. Once again, scriptures and stories tucked deep into my heart took on a fresh significance. Dying to self, relying on Him and the family and friends He'd surrounded me with: these gifts were new every day.

Eventually, as my spiritual vision grew, my physical vision began to sharpen. Instead of a couple of weeks, it took months. When my sight recovered, I would stop and pray a thank-you every time a street sign or leaf came into focus. I still do. Just today I saw a bright red cardinal outside my window and thanked God I could see such a beautiful slice of creation. I do have some complications related to my eyes, and they may never be fully resolved. But I am still hopeful and grateful, both for what I've learned in the journey and for coming out the other side.

Mom Genes

I've often said that it's harder to shop for a flattering pair of jeans than it is to find a swimsuit. I've experimented with many denim trends in an effort to find a solution, with many epic fails along the way. But while I've definitely *worn* "mom jeans" at some unfortunate points in my life, after twenty-three years of marriage, I've learned that I don't seem to have the mom *genes*.

When people meet me and Sheldon, the small talk almost always involves them asking how many kids we have. When I say, "None," an awkward silence usually follows. Parenthood is such a point of connection for so many people, they don't know how to respond when they find out that's an experience I don't share. Should they be empathetic because the Breams desperately wanted children, pursued fertility treatments, and struck out? Are we heartless, selfish, career-driven individuals who hate kids? Neither is true, and it's often challenging to find the words to describe our journey. I always worry I'll offend someone in the process, so I don't discuss it often.

As a kid, I didn't like being a kid myself. Other kids drove me bonkers. Why couldn't we all just hurry up and be adults? I wanted to stay up late, watch the TV shows I wanted to watch, eat what I wanted, and be free. It's not until you wind up with a mortgage, car payments, and hefty tax bills that you realize the only time you *were* free was when you were a kid.

In many ways, I came out of the womb an elderly person. I remember excitedly dressing up as an old woman for some costume event we were having at school. Who dresses up as a senior citizen when they're eight? To this day, I go crazy over older people like most people do over babies. I love hearing their stories and letting them know people care about who they are and what they've lived through. If you invite me to a party, and an aged friend or relative is also there, that's where you'll find me. They are my tribe!

From an early age, I somehow knew I didn't want children of my own. Whenever my mom would get frustrated and tell me what a handful I was, I'd glibly reply, "Well, YOU decided to have me." Meanwhile, my friends loved playing house and dreaming about the day their baby dolls would be the real thing. I remember getting a Baby Alive doll one Christmas. She actually "ate" food and soiled her diapers. It was all very overwhelming for me. "Baby, you're gonna have to slow down on the diapers because I've got other stuff to do," I would lecture the doll. "Stuff that's actually fun."

For decades I've hesitated to voice these thoughts because I don't often meet other women who share them. I've prayed for loved ones who tearfully struggled on the path to parenthood, some of them never arriving where they hoped they would. We've rejoiced when friends got approved for adoptions and when families came together in unexpected ways. There was even a brief period in our early thirties when I seriously considered taking the plunge. Our friends' homes were filling up with precious babies. Shower invitations flooded in nearly every week, and we saw less and less of our friends as they transitioned from dinner dates to playdates. For a few months, Sheldon and I decided to let nature take its course. If we ended up pregnant, fantastic. If we didn't, also fine by me. Yet, even as we opened ourselves up to the possibility, I never started yearning for a child of my own, and I felt relief each month when I discovered I wasn't pregnant. We concluded that it wasn't meant to be and went back to a preventive stance.

Many, many times this decision has made me feel like an outsider. As the couples in our Sunday school class grew increasingly focused on their offspring, as is the natural course of things, I felt disapproval start to build when it became clear that I wasn't actively trying to get on the Mommy train. At one women's event in particular, I even tried articulating how I was feeling to a group of my peers.

"Don't you guys ever feel overwhelmed?" I asked.

"These are our *children*," one interjected. "You'd feel differently if you had your own." The rest of the group seemed to agree. It felt like they thought I was defective because I didn't share the urge to be a mother. I actually got up and left as quickly as I could. I was an outlier, and no one seemed to understand where I was coming from.

In my mind, I had given God a window for sending us a child. He didn't, so I no longer had to pretend like that was the only possible vision for my life. Besides, we'd heard enough "surprise baby" stories from our friends to know that if God meant us to have children, nothing we did to prevent it would matter. Sheldon himself had been a surprise, and I couldn't be more thankful for that!

So, how to articulate myself and find my place—in the church, in society, in the workplace? I've always had coworkers who toil under the same long hours as me while also managing to serve as dedicated mothers. I'm not going to lie, I don't know how they do it. And every stay-at-home mother I know is a veritable Superwoman. I stand in awe of their ability to multitask, often on very little sleep. That truly seems like the most challenging job in the universe.

Pouring love into little lives, watching their failures and successes, seeing this amazing world through their eyes of wonder, hearing them say "I love you"—I have no doubt there's nothing like it. People often ask us if we'll miss that part of life, and it's sometimes made me question myself. But at the end of every bit of soul-searching is this: parenting is a task that deserves your full commitment, and I have no desire to be a parent myself.

I love the work I do, and it truly feels like a calling. One that often means long hours, days, weeks, and months—often with an unpredictable travel schedule. I feel great purpose in chasing the truth and making sure my viewers get all sides of the story. It's exhausting and deeply rewarding, much like I imagine parenthood is to those who know it is their calling.

I believe it's such an honorable and exhausting task that you have to have enormous enthusiasm about doing it. I often felt pressure from friends, family, and church leaders to "get with the program." But isn't it possible my path is different from most women's? Maybe I've been wired differently? I find enormous joy and pride in my godchildren and nieces and nephews. Throughout our lives, Sheldon and I have had young people come to us in times of great need. We were humbled to be able to help when they needed someone.

I'm at peace with our decision, and I respect people across the spectrum who feel differently. I don't believe God gives us cookie-cutter lives that must follow a certain path. He has different assignments for all of us. There have been kid-free parts of our lives and seasons where someone needed us quite a bit. It's all had meaning and purpose for the Breams. None of this excuses those horrible high-waisted, pleated, frumpy mom jeans I once thought were flattering. For THAT, there's really no explanation . . .

What My Dog Taught Me About God

From the moment the furry little ball of chocolate sat shivering in my lap, I would've thrown myself in front of a semi-truck for our Mocha. She was a typical chocolate Lab puppy, meaning it was nearly impossible to take her for a walk without a dozen strangers gasping at her cuteness and begging to pet her.

Four years into our marriage, we had both thought it was time to add to our happy home. Unbeknownst to Sheldon, I was talking with a breeder about getting him his dream dog: a German shorthaired pointer puppy. Little did I know, Sheldon was already making plans of his own. It's a good thing we both confessed our Christmas surprises to each other before two pups showed up to decimate our town house. At many points during those early months, one tiny beast felt like more than enough.

If you've had the joy of raising a dog, you know that their sheer adorableness is the only thing that keeps them alive during their first year on this planet. Mocha was a typical Lab, chewing on everything in sight—including the legs of my grand piano and a full-sized chair that she somehow ripped to shreds. We were maniacal in following the puppy discipline manuals: no people food, no jumping up on guests (even when they pretend to love it), and no random barking. Mocha was the star of her obedience class, with a cozy crate and plenty of vet-approved toys and snacks. But accidents happen, especially when you start giving them small doses of freedom.

It wasn't until several years into her life that I realized my dog could teach me a lot about God. Sheldon and I wanted her to be perfect twenty-four seven, but she had a free (and very strong) will. We knew what was best for her, but that didn't stop her from occasionally disobeying and running off like a crazed wild boar. Did it make me stop loving her? Not even close. It made me want to make her understand why we set certain rules and expectations. Those were only to protect her so that she could enjoy all the other awesome stuff out there like long hikes, diving into tempting ponds, and chasing tennis balls until we gave up. (She never did!)

I'll never forget the sheer terror of one of the first times we allowed Mocha a little free time outside her crate. She was only a few months old. We went out for a bit and were talking about adding a stop at the bookstore on the way home. Side note: Sheldon's nightmare is a bookstore, mostly because I'd take up residence in one if it was legal. It's never a "quick" visit, so it's a good thing Sheldon convinced me that we didn't need to go that night.

We arrived home as a storm was rolling in, anxious to see how our pup had done with her little bit of freedom, but we thought it strange when she didn't greet us at the door. We called and called—"Mocha! Where are you?"—and our search became more frantic when she didn't come. After rushing around the house, we found our puppy trapped under the coffee table, her head swelled to the size of a basketball. She looked disoriented and was having trouble breathing.

I immediately burst into tears and dialed our vet—but no one answered. Late on a Friday night with a full-on tropical storm now bearing down on us, the only emergency vet open was a good thirty minutes away.

Normally Sheldon drives when we're together, but something that night compelled me to get behind the wheel. He held her in the backseat, trying to soothe her (and me) while I sped down the highway sobbing and trying desperately to see through not only my tears, but also the pounding rains. In that moment, I realized that no matter how many times Mocha disobeyed or disappointed us I would move heaven and earth to save her. There was no question I loved her unconditionally, just like my Heavenly Father loves me.

We never found out what caused Mocha's allergic reaction, but with some medication and TLC, she was back to normal within a couple of days. And by *normal*, I mean looking for trouble . . .

When we lived in Charlotte, we had a large backyard that trailed off into a tiny, wooded ravine with a little stream running through it. On the other side of the water, it jutted up to a steep hill that eventually wound up in another neighbor's yard. While Mocha knew the boundaries of that yard, she sometimes found it irresistible to barrel right past them.

I was working a morning shift at the time, so I would come home midday—all dressed up from the office—and get Mocha outside as quickly as possible for a potty break. She was usually happy to do her business and hurry back in for a treat. We had it down to a science. Until we didn't . . .

One day, my mother-in-law and sister-in-law had come for a visit, and Mocha decided this would be a great time to misbehave. As they watched from our back deck, Mocha looked at me—looked back at them—and decided to make a run for it. My yelling and commands fell on deaf ears. She was determined and she wasn't looking back. With my in-laws laughing from the deck, I took off after Mocha in heels and hose. I had to traipse through the water, the briars, the downed branches—and I wasn't even close to catching her. I knew what was next: scaling that incline.

Covered in mud (and torn hose) from the knees down, I finally caught sight of my wayward pooch as she approached the neighbor's house. The neighbor came out to help me corral her, but he was unable to disguise the shock on his face when he saw me in full hair and TV makeup, my shirt untucked, sweating and furious. I grabbed Mocha's collar and dragged her home—down that incline, through the muddy stream, and finally emerging on the other side, where my thoroughly amused in-laws had watched the whole thing. Was I steaming mad? Was Mocha in big trouble? Was I still madly in love with her? Yes to all.

It makes me think about the times I run away from all the good things God has planted in my life, only because I think something even better is out there. He's given me the Garden of Eden and I'm out looking for a taco stand. God has chased me many more times than I ever went after our wayward lab. But no matter how far I go off track, He's pursuing me—through the mud and the briars—to bring me back home safely.

Even as she reached the end of her sixteen years of life, Mocha was still full of independence and curiosity. Many days she would pull and struggle against the leash, even though the only reason I kept her so close was to protect her from things she could no longer see clearly. It was a journey, one in which I never gave up on her and she always came home . . . eventually.

There Are No Coincidences

The first time I heard about Twitter, I truly thought, *How arrogant to think anyone wants to hear your thoughts about anything in a hundred forty characters*. Slowly, though, I got sucked in. That anyone, anywhere in the world can spout their original (and sometimes not-so-original) thoughts into a public space for consumption is a novel concept.

The dark side of it, of course, is that people can do all this anonymously, and they often do so with great venom. I'm convinced that people wouldn't say 99 percent of the nastiness they spew on social media if they were standing face-to-face with the person who's the target of their insults. And while the vast majority of the interactions I have on Twitter and Facebook are positive, the vile, hateful attacks are the ones that stick with you. My skin has gotten much thicker over the last decade, mostly by necessity. When people insult my clothes, my intelligence, or my appearance, I remind myself that those attacks often come from people who've never actually watched my work. They just hate *where* I work. The Twitter mute button is a glorious thing.

The insults that sting most are the ones that bear some modicum of truth—when we've missed something on a story or could have done a better job with our coverage. I don't know if you've ever had complete strangers critique your work and blast their opinions to the world, but it can be a tough thing to digest—especially when they're right. All this to say, I've got a pretty jaded view of social media and the way in which it's given so many people a license to take our culture to a new low.

All that changed, though, one week in March of 2018. That Sunday morning, our pastor had preached about praying for really big things—things so beyond your own skills and resources that only God could get the credit. Shortly after church, I got an email from a gentleman I'd met on a plane weeks earlier. He told me his young nephew, Emilio, was dying and had only one wish. Emilio wanted to get a personal greeting from one of the actors in *The Avengers*. Did I know anyone connected to the movie franchise?, the uncle asked. Sadly, no. To be honest, I didn't even know what an Avenger was!

As I stood in my kitchen contemplating the request, I thought about that morning's sermon. Sure, I didn't have any Hollywood connections, but the power of prayer is bigger than any earthly obstacle. So I told Emilio's uncle I'd give it a try. I whipped up a tweet asking for help finding an Avenger, said a prayer for big things, and sent it out into the online world.

> "Need your help Twitterverse—trying to help a young boy who is dying. He probably has just days and all he wants is a greeting from one of the Aveng-

> ers. If you have a celeb connection, please let me know. Otherwise, could you help out with a RT? Thank you in advance!"

Within hours I got a private message from CNN anchor Jake Tapper. "I'm friends with Paul Rudd, who plays Ant-Man. Would that count?"

I asked Emilio's uncle if Ant-Man qualified. He did! I connected Jake with Emilio's family, and Paul sent a series of video greetings. I checked back on the original tweet and was stunned to see the thousands of retweets piling up. Meghan McCain sent me a contact and then others started coming in—producers, agents, and other people who were actually part of the Avengers' world. Chris Evans, who plays Captain America in the movies, was next to send a message to Emilio. From there, it turned into an avalanche.

As I got updates on Emilio's condition, I asked his uncle whether the boy had faith and was at peace with what he was facing. He assured me that Emilio was wise beyond his years and covered in prayers. I told him I was praying for them around the clock. I also learned about the family's efforts to start a foundation so that other parents facing terrifying diagnoses like Emilio's would have somewhere to turn for information.

By Monday I was fielding personal messages from Paul Bettany and Benedict Wong. Both sent personal messages of encouragement. Zachary Levi asked whether it would be possible to Skype a call with young Emilio, who was quickly fading. When that didn't work, Zachary quickly recorded a heartfelt video. We tried to channel the messages to him and his family as quickly as we could. My colleague Ellison Barber started working her connections too.

At one point, I worried that these movie stars would make the connection between me and my work at Fox and choose not to get involved over a political disagreement. That never happened. Everyone who got the message in time scrambled to get the details from me and put together something for Emilio. Some of them did so in character. Others took selfie videos from wherever they happened to be and sent messages of inspiration and encouragement.

I never got the chance to meet Emilio, but at one point his uncle sent me an audio recording made from his hospital bed—a thank-you for the messages that had poured in. He sounded so weak, yet so overjoyed that Avengers from around the globe were personally taking time to reach out to him.

When I got word that Emilio passed away Wednesday morning, I grieved alongside his family. But in that moment, it was comforting to know that the world had gotten to light up his hospital room during the last few days of his life. I couldn't believe that first tweet would bring together thousands of people and dozens of celebrities, whom I had no way of connecting with outside of a miracle.

That week, I had gotten dozens of calls and messages from reporters and media outlets covering the story. It made me realize how hungry everyone is for some positive news these days—even though this particular story ended up so bittersweet. In each interview I told them the story about my pastor and how I had prayed for something so big that

I could never get the credit when it actually happened. Most publications didn't include that part of the story, but it truly is the most important for me.

A young boy had launched a tidal wave of goodwill and kindness, giving thousands of people the chance to witness a miracle and share God's goodness with the world. From that chance flight sitting by Emilio's uncle to the sermon I heard that Sunday morning, I don't believe any of it was a coincidence, and it certainly reminded me that social media—like so many other things in life—can be used as a force for good.

Witnessing History

For more than a decade, my life has revolved around what's happening at the US Supreme Court. When I first landed the assignment to cover the court for Fox, I had no idea how much I *didn't* know. Unlike Capitol Hill, which has more leaks than your average colander, the court is nearly impenetrable for journalists. I didn't know the details of the justices' private conferences, how they decide who writes which opinion, or what happens when they get an emergency filing.

The problem was twofold. The existing press corps didn't exactly roll out the red carpet for the newbie. (It's a demanding job, and they had work to do.) More important, I didn't want to ask questions and give any hint that I didn't have things totally under control.

I stumbled through the first cases I covered, including a terrorism trial involving the detention center at Guantánamo Bay. The case was so confusing, I still get lost in the legal documents whenever I revisit it. It had ping-ponged through the federal court system for years before finally landing at the Supreme Court for a 5-4 decision. It's one of the only cases I still worry I didn't adequately communicate to our viewers.

Slowly but surely I started to get the flow of what happens behind closed doors at the court: why one emergency filing goes to Justice Alito but another goes to Justice Kagan and how to cover an hour-long oral argument without a recording device. To this day, you must surrender any and all electronic gadgets before entering the courtroom, and you'll go through at least two metal detectors before you get there. For reporters, whose job is to run out and report every detail as soon as the chief justice bangs his gavel, the arrangement can be challenging.

On days when I'm covering a case, I always take the prep notes I've gathered, a legal pad, and at least two pens. (Anything less is a rookie mistake—you will run out of ink at the most critical point in the arguments.) On big case days, assigned seats are reserved months in advance and chairs are jammed in so tight you have to suck it in until you get where you're going. There's always a palpable sense that you're about to witness history. No cameras or livestreams are allowed in the court, so very few people ever get to experience what happens in that beautifully gilded room. They're counting on the media to let them know.

Many of the reporters crammed in on the most important argument days are sitting behind pillars and curtains blocking their view. Each of the justices' voices is unique, but it does take a while to get to know who's talking when you can't see anyone. It's a tricky beat to cover, and after a decade, I still feel like there are things I've yet to master.

The real excitement—or panic—comes at the end of the term, which runs October to June. That's when most of the landmark decisions are announced, often after months of public arguments and behind-the-scenes negotiations. Generally the justices will vote on a case the Friday after it's heard, but that's just the beginning of the story. As the justices write the majority and dissenting opinions, they're often still hoping to sway hearts and minds and change their colleagues' votes. It happens.

We know the days we will get opinions from the court, but no one knows *which* cases will be released (unless it's the final day of the term and you can figure out which ones are left by process of elimination). Reporters squeeze into the court's public information office and wait for the clock to strike 10:00 a.m., the set-in-stone time when the court releases new decisions. The first hint is the number of sealed boxes. One is a slow day. Two or three mean either multiple opinions or a smaller number that are very detailed and lengthy. It's an educated guessing game.

Most networks will have reporters stationed live at cameras on the sidewalk outside the court, and interns in the press office who deliver the reports. Over time, the whole process has morphed into something called "The Running of the Interns." Interns and other young staffers jockey to take on the challenge of getting those hard-copy opinions from inside the court, where running is strictly forbidden, to the live positions out on the sidewalk as quickly as possible. The competition is fierce, and the bragging rights last all summer long.

For years, I would grab the opinions from the press office and run them out to the camera myself. As a world-class micromanager, I didn't trust anyone to get the urgency of the task at hand. Upon arriving at the camera, I would catch my breath, digest the opinion in my hand as quickly as possible, and then try to make sense of it all on live TV within seconds.

I distinctly remember one of the first times I ran the gauntlet. We were awaiting a major Second Amendment decision. I wanted to be the first reporter to break the news, and I was worried about how quickly I'd be able to break down the case.

Clear as day, I remember grabbing the very long opinion and starting the run. As I rounded one corner, I glanced down to see that Justice Scalia had authored the majority decision. Given his love of hunting and stories about how he used to carry a rifle on the New York subway system, I immediately knew where the case was going. I was right. Years later, my friend and former colleague Greta Van Susteren gave me a great additional tip: often you can learn more about the outcome of a case by looking to see who wrote the dissent. Knowing who lost tells you just as much as, if not more than, who won.

There is enormous pressure to get things first on days like this at the court. With every media outlet camped outside and cameras set in place hours before the decisions come, reporters arrive on the scene hoping to be the first to report the ruling live on their network. It's tough to sleep the night before because opinions are filled with nuance and can easily exceed a hundred pages in complex cases. I prepare by digging through my legal pads filled with notes, rereading the reports I filed when the cases were argued, and often reviewing the transcript as well.

I did all those things as we awaited the historic ruling on the constitutionality of the Affordable Care Act, or "Obamacare." The country was deeply divided over the legislation, which passed without a single Republican vote. Many believed it would make health care more accessible to all Americans and that they wouldn't have to break ties with their existing doctors. Others argued it was an unconstitutional government takeover of (by some estimates) one-sixth of the country's economy.

Cases normally get a single hour for argument, but the justices had granted hours of arguments on this particular case, which had spread over three days. I tossed and turned the night before we knew the case was coming—the final day of the term in June 2012. We set up a line of communication from a producer stationed inside the courtroom to start digging into the decision while I awaited the hard copy outside at my live camera position on the sidewalk. His voice was routed into my ear so that we could compare notes.

That morning, the crowds outside the court were substantial and energized, waiting for any hint about the future of Obamacare. As Chief Justice John Roberts started reading his majority opinion, opponents of the law who were sitting in the courtroom were gleeful. They believed they had won and that the individual mandate did not survive the legal challenge.

That was the same message I was getting from my producer reading through the opinion from inside the court's pressroom. Out on the sidewalk, that appeared to be the case to me at first blush as well. The first portion of the chief's opinion ticked through all the reasons Obamacare did *not* meet constitutional scrutiny. It wasn't until dozens of pages into the nearly-two-hundred-page opinion that the truth surfaced: the court held that the law operated as a tax and was a valid use of Congress's taxing authority.

But it was too late. Feeling confident in the initial assessment, I announced on-air that it looked like the mandate had been found unconstitutional. It took only a couple of minutes to realize that I was wrong, and I wanted the ground to swallow me whole. We weren't the only network to make the mistake, but it was my nightmare come true. I had gotten something of grave importance wrong on the air and there was no way to undo it. In the blistering sun I could feel the sweat dripping down my back as I quickly tried to make things right.

Greta was right. Had I turned to the dissent I would have seen that all four of the court's conservative-leaning justices—Scalia, Kennedy, Thomas, and Alito—had jointly signed the dissent. Had I looked at the dissent before making my assessment, I would've known that the mandate had survived. It was a confusing mishmash of decisions, and I dropped the ball.

Sources later told me that both the liberal and conservative wings of the court had spent time thinking Roberts was on their side. While almost everyone thought Justice Kennedy was the "swing vote" going into the decision, I'm told he never wavered. He was always of the mind that Congress had overstepped its constitutional powers in passing the ACA. He continued to lobby Roberts, and at one point thought he might succeed. He reached out to the other conservatives, many of whom had left for various obligations, and urged them to get back to Washington immediately to meet with Roberts. At some point during those conversations, they realized Roberts was not going to be convinced and banded together to write their joint dissent.

I literally felt like I couldn't get out of bed the next day. The very worst thing I could imagine doing as a reporter— I'd done. My coworkers and friends were encouraging and empathetic. But every time someone reached out to say, "It's going to be okay. People respect you. We all make mistakes," the wound just kept getting ripped open. I reached out to a fellow media colleague who'd also gotten it wrong, and we commiserated about staying in our pajamas and eating ice cream until people forgot about us. It was years ago, but the pain is just as vivid as the day I made that mistake.

Like everything in life, you have to take lessons from the things that are painful—or else they're just pointless. I cover the court differently now because of what happened that day. And despite one of my worst fears being realized, the sun did come up the next morning. My loved ones didn't abandon me, though I did have to talk them down from exacting revenge after some public figures decided to publicly mock and belittle me. Most important, my Heavenly Father knew the pain and humiliation I was feeling and comforted me as I began the slow work of putting the failure behind me.

One of the most interesting parts of my job involves getting to know the justices personally as the opportunities present themselves. Justice Stephen Breyer hosts a lunch with a number of reporters in May or June of each year, for an off-the-record chat about life and what's going on at the court. As I walked to the lunch one day in 2015, I got a phone call that stopped me in my tracks. "We've found something troubling and we're going to need to talk to you about scheduling your surgery. How soon can you come in?"

The doctor explained that my breast biopsy did not look good and I needed surgery as soon as possible. With tears streaming down my face as traffic raced by, I didn't even consider canceling the Breyer lunch. I felt it would be rude and I'd have to answer questions about why I didn't show up. So I went, even though I couldn't digest a single word of the conversation.

Weeks earlier I'd had a mammogram that showed a troublesome spot the doctors wanted to examine further. I stayed for the next level of screening and soon got the word that I'd need a needle biopsy. Like women around the world every day, I was thrown onto an unknown path filled with endless questions: how big was the trouble spot, was I going to lose my breast, was I going to die young, why can't anyone answer these questions RIGHT NOW?!

The biopsy? I'm going to be straight with you. It was both stressful and painful, though the doctors and nurses who walked me through the process were as clear and compassionate as they could be through the procedure. To anyone dreading a mammogram, I say don't hesitate. It is not like getting a luxurious massage, but it's also much better than a root canal. For me, it's never been painful—just uncomfortable. Do it now.

For days, I had jumped every time my phone rang. What if I was in a meeting? What if I was asleep or at the gym?

Why couldn't we just schedule the call? Instead, I was on a street corner alone crying my eyes out while I tried to pull it together and head to an important lunch acting as if I hadn't just been punched in the gut.

On the recommendation of a colleague who'd been through—and beaten—a much more serious breast cancer challenge, Sheldon and I made an appointment to see a top-notch surgeon. I will always be grateful for that colleague's calming, encouraging words through those days.

June is my Super Bowl, when all the big decisions come down from the court. I didn't want to miss a minute of it. I was torn between wanting to get the offending tissue out of my body as quickly as possible and not missing the most important weeks of my job. My surgeon and my husband quickly overruled my plans to delay the surgery and it was set for June 16.

If you've had surgery you know what that day is like. You've fasted—so you're starving and probably a bit on edge. My procedure was delayed again and again, leaving me to listen to the radio that was playing in the waiting room. Donald Trump was toying with running for president, the host said, and had a big announcement planned for that day. I'd interviewed him only weeks before, but really didn't think he was planning to run. In fact, I was so unconvinced that he actually pulled me aside after the interview and said, "I don't think you're taking me seriously." Busted.

Finally the time came for my IV. The resident looked exactly like my little brother, Eddy, and seemed a tad nervous. He made several attempts at finding the vein, and I tried to keep a smile on my face rather than freaking out and putting even more pressure on him. When my surgeon peeked in and saw the growing panic on my face, she quickly took over and we were on our way.

As I began to awake from the anesthesia—that window when you most certainly should avoid blurting things out, but seem to have no filter whatsoever—I remember mumbling to the nurses about the crazy dream I'd had, "Donald Trump running for president! Wouldn't that be so funny?!"

One of the nurses replied, "Oh, that's actually happening." I giggled and fell back to sleep.

A couple of my colleagues noticed my absence during those critical Supreme Court days and reached out to see what was wrong. I was very hesitant to share because, once again, I was awaiting results and felt very vulnerable. As I sat propped up at home in my robe, I watched those mornings at the Supreme Court from afar—hoping and praying that nothing earth-shattering would happen while I was away. Sheldon had to be away on a long-planned trip so my mom was there waiting on me hand and foot. She was much more curious about taking a look at my wound than I was. I remember my surgeon telling me that there would eventually be a day when I wouldn't see it every single time I looked in the mirror when I stepped out of the shower.

I was determined to get back to the court as quickly as I could without anyone knowing I was in recovery. I didn't want the questions or the pity. I wanted to work. When I left the hospital, the doctors gave me mini ice packs to place alongside my bandages as my wound healed those first couple of days. In my case, this turned out to have an unexpected benefit. The long, late-June days at the court can be blisteringly hot, and when I returned to my post there a few days after surgery, the ice packs in my bra were my secret weapon.

On that day, June 26, 2015, the Supreme Court sent a shock wave through the country by legalizing same-sex marriage in all fifty states. The crowd awaiting the decision was massive. As supporters of the ruling began to celebrate, my friend Peter Doocy told me I should take a selfie to capture what that moment was like.

When I posted it on social media, people accused me of being either devastated or joyous over the court's decision. It's not my job to share my personal opinion on the air, so I didn't offer any explanation. But when I see that picture now, I think of someone with ice packs hidden in her bra, so grateful to be alive and healthy and doing the job I love. And my surgeon was right. I almost never think of that scar on my breast when I look in the mirror.

Lessons from the Trail

When people ask me if covering the actual seat of government makes me want to run for office, I simply sigh. Having seen it up close, it's nothing like I used to think it would be, in ways both good and bad. I fear that the nastiness and mudslinging and inaction on Capitol Hill is keeping decent men and women from dragging their good names into the fight—not to mention their precious family members. There are smart, well-intentioned people on both sides of the aisle, but watching the political process up close can often be demoralizing—at best.

Even at the Supreme Court, which works to be apolitical, some of the biggest recent fireworks have had nothing to do with legal decisions and everything to do with *who* was going to be hearing them. I've covered four Supreme Court confirmation battles, but nothing prepared me for just how contentious the battle over Justice Brett Kavanaugh got. Before he'd ever been named, several key voices on the left made it clear they would oppose any pick made by President Trump. Yet, with a sterling résumé and support from across the ideological aisle, it seemed Kavanaugh would have a relatively smooth confirmation journey.

But from day one of his original hearing, it quickly became evident this wasn't going to be business as usual. As the Senate Judiciary Committee Chairman Chuck Grassley began his opening statement, a volley of objections from Democrats on the committee rolled in. I was reporting from a skybox in the hearing room and scrambled to the sliding glass panes so I could see what was happening for myself. Not long after, protesters sitting in the seats at the back of the room started popping up at regular intervals. Those seats were for the public, and US Capitol Police stood by ready to take out protesters who refused to quietly sit and watch the proceedings.

It was like nothing I'd ever seen before. One after another, they jumped up and yelled their objections. Very quickly, they were escorted out and arrested by security. By the third day, Kavanaugh and the senators no longer batted an eyelash when a new protester erupted. Finally, the hearings wrapped and the committee moved forward with plans to vote on the nominee. Almost no one thought Kavanaugh had any real worries until days later, when the ranking member on the committee, Senator Dianne Feinstein, announced that she'd received a letter outlining serious allegations against Kavanaugh and referred it to the FBI. While the author of the letter said she wished to remain anonymous, Dr. Christine Blasey Ford soon became a household name.

What I saw unleashed over the next few weeks was astonishing, a new low in this country's political discourse. There were murder and rape threats against nearly all the key players, including family members and Senate staffers.

People on all sides were dragged through the mud, and protesters filled the halls and hounded lawmakers to the point that they needed armed security to get to and from their offices so they could vote. I feel safe in saying that many lives tangled up in the controversy will never be the same.

I worked diligently to stay in touch with all the legal teams involved, to provide our viewers the very latest as it came in, and to report objectively. As a woman—and as a lawyer—I have plenty of opinions about what transpired. As an American, I can only hope we find our way back to seeing people with whom we disagree as human beings.

I've had a lot of adventures covering politics, from city councils to the White House. The campaign trail is an exhausting place—a gauntlet for only the truly determined. I'm not sure most people have a realistic picture of what it truly means to run. The constant fund-raising will wear out even the most determined candidates, and you'd sure better like people! Often constituents who've seen me interview their representative on TV will mail me reams of papers, hoping I can funnel them to their lawmaker. From alien conspiracy theories to demands that someone investigate their neighbor's clandestine hog-breeding operations, nothing surprises me anymore.

I've come to see the world of politics split into two groups: egomaniacs and servant-hearted people. There are some about whom the press corps says, only half joking, "The most dangerous place in Washington is between that person and a camera." On the other end of the spectrum are the workhorse members who never end up in the headlines, wear the same ties over and over again, and set aside time to take phone calls from their constituents. I'm sure many lawmakers have both qualities competing inside them at various times. After all, you have to be supremely confident to enter a world where you—and most everyone you care about—are going to be attacked and belittled, whether the accusations are true or not.

On the other hand, I do meet people in office who let that all slide off their backs. They feel a call or an obligation to serve, and they don't let the noise bother them (at least not too much). These people operate from a core set of principles, and they don't worry about making everyone happy. It often makes their party leadership insane because they can't control them through promises of committee assignments or fund-raising advantages. I'd like to think the Founders envisioned these scenarios and that's why they built so many checks and balances into our system.

Now what the campaign trail lacks in glamour, it makes up for in entertainment. There are always surprise announcements, a cast of characters, and travel drama. Back in 2011, I took part in one of the Fox News GOP primary debates. Bret Baier, Chris Wallace, Juan Williams, and I spent weeks preparing. It was my first major debate and I had no idea how painstaking the preparation would be. I loved every minute of it, but it requires mountains of research, sharpening questions over and over again, and negotiating with campaigns and candidates, all of whom have different demands about how the whole thing should go.

As we took to the stage in Greenville, South Carolina, I felt enormous pressure. Generally, if I do enough homework, I feel comfortable walking into any situation. This felt exponentially different.

"You ready?" asked my boss, Bill Sammon, who has run more marathons than I can count.

"Honestly?" I replied. "I think if I could head outside and run a full marathon right this second it might begin to take the edge off the nerves I'm feeling." It was showtime.

Debates are carefully choreographed affairs, from the topics of discussion to the commercial breaks, the amount of time given to each candidate, and the efforts to wrangle an unruly audience. The planning is exceptionally detailed, but once it's all set in motion it's up to the candidates to break through.

That night the crowd was rowdy and responsive, letting the candidates know exactly how they felt about their answers. My questions focused on health care costs, immigration, and social issues like abortion and stem cell research. When I talked to my dad on the phone afterward, he said he thought Herman Cain had easily "won the whole shootin' match." We had an early finish, so I headed back to the hotel and crashed.

The next morning most of the Fox crew boarded a flight from Greenville back to Dulles airport just outside DC. I've been flying since I was just a little kid, and the experience has never bothered me. That all changed on May 6, 2011.

The pilot warned us that we were facing a bumpy ride. It wasn't a large plane, and very quickly it felt like we were being tossed around like rag dolls. There were those sudden, large drops when you feel as if the plane is simply free-falling to the ground. I began to panic, as did several others on the plane. My nose started to bleed, and the man next to me quickly came to my aid. Thank goodness he was a doctor. He tried to calm me down, but I could see the worry in his eyes too. Things were only getting worse. The doctor engaged me in conversation, I think, in an effort to distract both of us. I found out his wife was expecting their first child and he was suddenly very insistent that he had to survive the flight and get back to her. Once I saw the fear in his eyes and heard it in his voice, I knew I wasn't overreacting.

The flight seemed to go on for days, but when we finally landed at Dulles, I was a mess of bloody tissues and smeared makeup, shaking like a leaf. I had never been so happy to touch solid ground. Much (much) later I was able to joke about the news reports that would've told the story of our crash. "Fox anchors Bret Baier and Chris Wallace were on board, along with some reporter named Sharon Green." There was no crash that day, but I instantly doubted I would ever be able to get onto a plane again.

For years, I always flew with clenched fists, digging into the armrests, often praying (sometimes tearfully) from the moment we took off to the moment we landed. I hated everything about flying, but I had places to go and I refused to let my fear shut down my life. My brother is a pilot, so he's often talked me through my worst-case scenarios and assured me that planes are built for turbulence. I started to feel better once I read an article that said the last time a plane actually crashed because of turbulence complications was in 1969—before I was born!

I once asked my dear friend, the late Charles Krauthammer, for advice. He was a trained psychiatrist, so I hoped his expert opinion would make all the difference. He told me his wife, Robyn, hated to fly too. "So what do you do?" I asked, hoping for a miracle cure.

With his trademark smile, the good doctor said, "We get to the airport plenty early . . ."

"Yes???" I asked expectantly.

"Then," he said, "we give ourselves plenty of time to get settled in and drink a few glasses of wine."

"That's it?!" I replied.

Charles simply chuckled, and said, "That's it."

Thankfully, much of my work travel happens on trains and in cars. I've built up plenty of points and free rides on the Amtrak train running between New York and DC. In stark contrast to airplanes, I find it nearly impossible to stay awake on trains. The steady rhythm and quiet hum make my eyelids feel like warm molasses. There's no stopping the slumber!

Most of the places we go end up requiring driving at some point. I spent several weeks one fall covering a US Senate race in West Virginia. You have to drive just about everywhere, and in this case, "everywhere" included places so remote that our giant satellite truck had trouble picking up a decent signal. Most candidates keep up the pace of a professional athlete. I remember chasing Senator Joe Manchin all throughout the West Virginia mountains. We cycled through church gatherings, VFWs, state fairs, and BBQs—sometimes all in a single day.

On one particular stretch of ping-ponging around the Mountain State, my producer, Jake Gibson, and I were driving late into the night so that we could check in to our hotel and start the next day at the site of the first event. We were starving and there was nothing in sight. Finally we spotted a Hardee's and I disregarded any rules I have about healthy eating. I have to say, curly fries are a thing of beauty when you're starving to death on the campaign trail.

A couple of hours later we pulled into our hotel, ready to quickly check in to our rooms and collapse for a bit of sleep. A bellman hurried out to help me with my luggage and he couldn't quit staring at my chest. I thought it was unprofessional, but I was so exhausted I thought I'd let it go. Then I got the same treatment from the valet. What was this, some kind of hotel full of perverts?! I was not amused. Finally, Jake met me in the lobby, took one look at me, and asked why I was wearing a french fry on my lapel. In what became known as "the curly fry brooch incident," I could only laugh at myself and how unglamorous this job can really be.

And then there's Iowa. The people are incredibly nice and also exceptionally plugged in to politics. But you will never visit a place that is colder or windier than Iowa is in January. Reporters stand outside in that weather, and it's no joke. I am energized by covering caucuses, primaries, and campaigns, but I cry just a little when I realize I'm headed to Iowa during the winter. At one point in 2012, the freezing wind was so brutal that my microphone and earpiece connection would only function for minutes at a time. I would stand inside the door of the hotel, get everything turned on, and wait for the commercial break to end. Then, right before we went live, I bolted outside to the camera, got everything connected, and braced myself for just a few minutes in the howling wind. After my report, I'd run right back inside.

I was mocked for wearing earmuffs on-air, but I make zero apologies for the survival strategies I was forced to employ.

During the 2016 caucuses, the weather seemed milder in Iowa. As part of the campaign experience, top contenders try to show up at as many of the larger caucus meetings as they can. I was stationed at an auditorium where several candidates were expected to drop in, and the buzz when security came through the door was off the charts.

There's always a moment of hesitation as the crowd waits to see who's shown up. When then-candidate Trump and the future First Lady walked through the door, people shouted, "He's here! Trump showed up! She's with him too!" Mrs. Trump was a striking presence, looking like she'd stepped straight off the cover of a high fashion magazine in an elegant red dress and matching coat. They both shook hands and worked the room as the future president made his way to the stage.

Based on the crowd's response, then-candidate Trump wasn't the most popular contender to show up that night—an honor that would've gone to Ben Carson—but he did seem like the most determined. I don't know if he or the First Lady had spent much time in Iowa before he got serious about running, but they both worked to connect with people and convince the savvy Iowans they were in it to win it.

Once you get to the party political conventions themselves, the entire experience feels like it's been put on steroids. You're usually away from home for the better part of a month, scraping together quarters to use hotel laundry facilities and eating whatever you can get your hands on. Each network has its own workplace strewn with cables and wires of every shape and size. Often, a full TV set has been built so you can broadcast right from that space. The coverage runs for nearly twenty-four hours a day, and most of the employees are lucky to get a hotel room within thirty miles. The schedule doesn't leave much time for sleep (or laundry), but it's thrilling to be there witnessing history. At the RNC convention, everyone wants to snap photos and get autographs with Fox personnel. Not so much at the DNC, but most people know you're there to do a job. As part of the news division, it's straight down the middle for me—just the facts.

In 2016, I was standing in the typically monstrous line for one of the women's bathrooms at the DNC when someone spotted "Fox News" on the media badge we were required to wear for access to the floor. "Why are you even here?" she said angrily. "You're all propaganda, not news."

Before I could politely defend myself, a producer from one of the other mainstream cable networks did it for me. "She's a member of the media, just like I am. She's a straight news reporter, and you need to stop hassling her." Thank you!

I remember watching Hillary Clinton's speech from the floor of the DNC that night. I'd given up on heels after eighteen hours on the clock, so there I sat in my running shoes with some snacks I'd snuck in in my purse. As I listened that night and watched the balloons fall, I snapped several photos and took video on my phone, convinced that I was watching the next president of the United States take her first victory lap.

A little more than three months later, having been advised that the exit polls showed almost no chance for Donald

Trump to win the presidency, I watched through the night as state after state offered a new electoral surprise. I think it finally hit me when Ohio went red. I had spent a lot of time compiling lists of the possible candidates Hillary would be likely to select to fill the late Justice Scalia's seat on the Supreme Court. Sometime in the wee hours of November ninth I thought to myself, *Donald Trump is going to fill that seat, not Hillary.* It was a revelation. Despite all the polls and punditry, he was really going to pull off what all the experts claimed he couldn't do: become the commander in chief.

If there's one thing this job has taught me, it's just how unpredictable life can be. Sometimes your camera dies just before your big moment to shine. Sometimes you score a nugget from a source who didn't intend to give away that much; other times you get passed over for a plum assignment or miss your deadline. But in all of it there is still this truth: what you do with it is up to you. How you view your circumstances and respond to them can shape the entire trajectory of your life. I choose to believe there is purpose in the pain and that most people really do have good intentions. Many may call me nothing but an overzealous Pollyanna, but trust me—I've been called much worse.

Acknowledgments

It was my Facebook followers who first told me how much they loved my zany stories and encouraged me to share them more broadly. Cait Hoyt at CAA was my cheerleader, the one who made me believe this book might actually happen one day! Editor Derek Reed patiently walked me through the creation process, gently guiding me as a novice author to a final book I hope you'll find both entertaining and encouraging. Campbell Wharton always put a smile on my face and gave me the boosts of enthusiasm I needed to get this done.

This labor of love wouldn't exist if I hadn't learned how to spin a tale from my parents, or without the unwavering support of my husband, Sheldon, who was forced to re-walk down memory lane more than once so I could get the details just right.

Jackie Harris and Olivia Metzger have fought on my behalf to help me get to the place where this book dream actually came true. My assistant and friend, Anna Willey, has hustled like no one ever before to make the juggling act that is my life as smooth a ride as it can be. My Coraggios and "Sorority" sisters, you are true support and your stories are safe with me.

To My Heavenly Father, thank you for your many gifts and blessings. May I use them to point people to your saving grace.

ABOUT THE AUTHOR

SHANNON BREAM joined Fox News Channel in 2007 and currently hosts *Fox News @ Night* (weekdays at 11:00 p.m.). Previously, she was the cohost of *America's Newsroom* and the network's Supreme Court correspondent. Beyond her current cohosting slot, she regularly guest hosts top-rated FNC programs such as *Special Report* and *Fox News Sunday*. She is a graduate of Liberty University, a former Miss Virginia and Miss Florida, and earned a Juris Doctorate with honors from Florida State University College of Law.